MW00471484

Photo: Emma-lee Hacker

THE OTHER SIDE OF ME

memoir of a bipolar mind

JULIE KRAFT

Copyright 2016 by Julie Kraft

THE OTHER SIDE OF ME
memoir of a bipolar mind

first edition

All rights reserved.
No part of this book may be reproduced or transmitted in any form or by any
means, electronic or mechanical, including photocopying, recording, or by
any information storage and retrieval system without the written permission
of the author, except where permitted by law.

Editor Janet G Henderson

dedicated with love.

To the millions of people living with mental illness and everyone living and loving alongside. May my journey be inspiring proof that there is hope, help, and an amazingly bright light at the end of the tunnel.

I used to think you had to be special for God to use you, but now I know you simply need to say *yes*.

-Bob Goff

"Yes."

-Yours truly

with gratitude.

To my husband and children, for loving and never leaving me. I love you.

To Jan, my dear friend and editor extraordinaire, for your willingness to edit, refine, and polish my memoir. I could not have crossed the finish line of this book-writing marathon without you.

To all those who have come into my life and played a part in this book coming to fruition, for your unconditional love and support. You have given me the courage to share my story.

To Germany, my sanctuary and safe haven, for giving me peace, clarity, and perspective—everything I needed to pour myself out onto paper.

And last, but never least,
To God, for giving me the gift of life itself—everything and everyone in it. May my journey and words be used by Him in ways I never could have imagined.

43

37

47

21

TABLE OF CONTENTS

foreword

Bribery and an Airbag   19

A Mug Shot and Some Barbie Dolls   21

setting the stage

Running in Rush Hour Naked   25

Let's Get Technical | Questions & Answers   28

An Awkward Introduction   37

growing up

A Little Girl and a Lot of Chaos   43

The Big City and Some Fraud   47

A Monobrow and a First Marriage   51

A Few Men and a Missed Memo   55

married life

Fate and Finding a Mate   59

A Worried Wife and a Young Mom   62

comic relief

A Full-Priced Fuel-Up   66

Dirty Laundry and Dishonesty   69

Off to Visit the Queen   72

A Root Canal and a Casserole   77

the life I was "living"

A Masked Woman   81

DEPRESSION

Granny Panties and Groceries   99

Irrational Fears and Overreactions   102

MANIA

A Superhero and a Shirt Sale   108

A Sunburn and Some Rice   110

Midnight Run   113

Damage and Destruction   121

Leave Me and Never Look Back   125

An Online Betrayal   126

getting help

The Breaking Point   129

A Psychiatrist and a Search Party   132

Pill Popping   135

135 113

77 99

180 179

153 174

heading in a new direction

Twenty Questions and a Seed Sown 137

Insurance Coverage Denied 140

Painting a New Picture 145

Out of the Closet and Off a Cliff 148

Checking My Motives 150

A Sensitive Soul and Some Rejection 151

Take Me to Church 153

instructions and advice

Suspicious Behaviour and Tough Love 160

Dig Deeper 162

Open Your Heart to Me 163

Unmasked 164

Cut Yourself Some Slack 167

Keeping Good Company 169

Take it Slow 170

gentle reminders

Getting and Giving Respect 174

Watch Your Mind and Your Mouth 176

the life I'm now living

Small Fish in a Big Pond 179

Here Comes the Sun 180

keeping it real

A Shocking Admission   186
A Baseball Game and a Bad Rash   188

hope and healing

Ending on a High Note   195

186

188 195

foreword
(not to be confused with *fast-forward*)

Bribery and an Airbag

If you're not my biased birth mother or a *heavily* bribed best friend, please don't stop reading. At least not for a few more seconds and sentences. Not only does it mean this book is now a bonafide published work, out in the *real* world, it means you're holding a modern day miracle. Trust me, if you had any idea how easily distracted I can be (a fly in the neighbourhood will do it), how low my insecurities often drag me, or the disarray my bipolar disorder can bring to my state of being, then you'd only be *starting* to grasp how incredible it is this book was finished. The temptation to abandon my literary efforts was constant. I resisted. Instead of giving in and giving up, I logged off social media, cast aside self-doubt, fought through, and finished.

"Write the book you want to read." Such great advice, and I've tried to follow it. As a nonreader (easily distracted, remember?), I knew any book I'd be capable of reading, one that could keep my attention in its entirety, in *chronological* order, might possibly leave anyone else hanging on for dear life, wishing it had been sold with a crash helmet and airbag in its binding. Any such book would, hopefully, appeal to others and never be in danger of being tucked away for a rainy day. So I've done my very best to write *that* book and create a rollercoaster read—heartbreaking, head-spinning, side-splitting, eye-opening—a literary ride to be remembered. Buckle up and brace yourself.

A Mug Shot and Some Barbie Dolls

From the outside looking in or from a quick glance at my social media mug shot, it might seem as if I have my act together. From a *far* distance, others could be duped into thinking I have a "Ken and Barbie" marriage, three well-mannered kids, and that my teeth-whitening strips are working. Losing a set of car keys or a game of Monopoly might appear to be the hardest knocks life has ever thrown my way. But that couldn't be further from reality.

My headshot was snapped with the help of a tripod and a self-timer, as I sat alone, smiling at a pile of dirty laundry. I was overwhelmed that afternoon, too anxious to leave my home, and all because of a dose of medication I'd *forgotten* to take. The only things that helped to brighten my mood and coffee-stained smile that day were the miraculous capabilities of my photo-editing software. The truth is, I *don't* have it all together. Not at all. I could have easily kept my reality under wraps for the rest of my life. But keeping my struggles hidden behind an airbrushed smile would have only perpetuated the myth that I had all my ducks in a row. Or even worse, made others feel as if they didn't.

In shame for decades, I kept this part of me hidden from everyone except those closest to me—the people I was convinced would never "out" me, betray me, or leave me. I kept everything behind closed doors. Until now. Every story has two sides. This is *The Other Side of Me*.

21

"Opening up to others is *always* a risk.

There is the terrifying fear that others won't handle us with care or guard our vulnerabilities with the fierceness they deserve."

The moment that you
feel that, just possibly,
you're walking down
the street *naked*,
exposing too much of
your heart and your mind,
and what exists on the inside,
showing too much of yourself,
that's the moment you may be
starting to get it right.

-Neil Gaiman

setting the stage

Running in Rush Hour Naked

Metaphorically speaking, for me, what I'm about to do is the equivalent of running down a highway, in rush hour, *naked*. So here goes nothing. Or absolutely everything. I have bipolar disorder. Yes, that *is* the official diagnosis the guys in the white coats have given me and yes, I believe them. Could I have my clothes back, please?

Fully aware of the perceptions of mental illness, I know that even whispering the word *bipolar* sends some people, and insurance companies, running for the hills. Unfortunately, the media often portrays *us folk* as crazy-eyed maniacs—the ones who disappear for days on end, bingeing on sex, drugs, and alcohol, and impulsively spending insane amounts of money we *don't* have. We become the headline story on the six o'clock news and front page of the local newspaper for all the *wrong* reasons. We are extremely effective at satisfying others' insatiable appetites for any train wreck that isn't their own. *Crazy* sells.

Unfortunately, telling someone that I have bipolar disorder isn't easy. It's not the sort of news I can subtly slide into supermarket small-talk or sidewalk conversation. Until writing this book, I'd only "stripped down" and divulged my diagnosis to a select few, most of whom, thank goodness, reacted to my revelation in the best possible ways—as if they were only hearing of bad gas or a recurring rash. They've always viewed my disorder as something I *have*, not something I *am*. It has never defined our relationships or me. To them, I've always been more than my mental illness. *So much more.*

The problem is, for so many years I didn't share any of those same sentiments. I desperately wanted to believe what my friends believed and see myself through their eyes, but was so far from being able to do so. I knew of the fear and judgment of mental illness and was aware that stigma and stereotypes existed. And not only did they exist, they thrived, in my *very own* mind. Yes, I shamefully admit that *I, too,* viewed bipolarity as something to be steered clear of and kept at a distance. That is, until *I* heard the words, "You have bipolar disorder." In that moment, everything changed. All of my negative perceptions suddenly shifted in my direction. The spotlight was on me, and without welcome.

Getting to a place of accepting and embracing my disorder wouldn't be easy, or happen overnight.

"Yes, I shamefully admit that *I*, *too*, viewed bipolarity as something to be steered clear of and kept at a distance."

Let's Get Technical

(for those reading this book for
more than just the jaw-dropping, juicy parts)

Before I write any further, it's probably a good idea to give an (amateur) overview of my disorder. *Please* know, I am not a neurologist, psychiatrist, or doctor, nor do I desire to be. And this book is not an encyclopedia, medical journal, or diagnostic manual, so please don't look to it as one.

Unbelievably, until writing this memoir, I was intentionally unaware of the "ins and outs" of my condition. "Pinning" and "posting" online always took priority over any searches of my disorder. Many might think I'm ignorant and irresponsible for not studying every angle of my "ailment"—for not learning about neurotransmitters and their purposes before starting to pop my little pink pills. So, for the sake of appearing educated and somewhat self-aware, allow me to toss in a few facts and explore the more technical side of things. Here is my best attempt to educate.

Bipolar disorder, previously known as ***manic depressive disorder*** until its name change in 1980, is a serious mental illness that brings unpredictable and extreme changes in mood, behaviour, and energy. These shifts range from depression to mania—the depths of despair up to cloud number nine, and everywhere in between. Whether during a single day or over the course of years, these swings extend far beyond what

28

would be considered "normal"—disrupting life at best, and threatening to destroy everything and everyone in their path at worst.

There are different types—*bipolar I, II, mixed state, rapid cycling,* and *cyclothymia*—each with different levels of severity and their own distinctive features. Depressive and manic episodes are some of the glaring signs of this condition, and exploring them in detail can help nail down a diagnosis. Unfortunately, bipolar disorder can present a series of symptoms which fit the mold of other mood disorders; the average person receives a misdiagnosis (or four) before being given an accurate assessment.

There are many different treatment paths to explore: medication, psychotherapy, electrotherapy, counselling, lifestyle changes, and more. For those who opt to go the medicinal route, cocktails of methodically mixed medications (mood regulators, antipsychotics, and antidepressants) are often prescribed in the hope of stabilizing moods (and relationships). Some folks have great success out of the gate, while others need to explore different options, tweak dosages, and wade through a sea of side effects.

But is bipolar a disease or a disorder? Is it a chemical imbalance or just the sign of an unsettled upbringing? What is the real cause? And is there a cure?

Q. **Is it all in my head? Is there something going on or off in my brain? A chemical misfiring, of sorts, that can't be fixed by a prayer, bouquet of roses, or passionate kiss?**

(Well, the fact that brain-tweaking medications have been proven to help stabilize moods, including my own, would strongly suggest the answer is "yes.")

A. "Experts believe bipolar disorder is partly caused by an underlying problem with specific brain circuits and the balance of brain chemicals called neurotransmitters. The brain chemical serotonin is connected to many body functions, such as sleep, wakefulness, eating, sexual activity, impulsivity, learning, and memory. Researchers believe that abnormal functioning of brain circuits that involve serotonin as a chemical messenger contribute to mood disorders, such as depression and bipolar disorder." *

*www.webmd.com/bipolar-disorder/guide/bipolar-disorder-causes?page=2)

Q. Is there a genetic predisposition to mental illness and bipolar disorder? Did I come by my condition honestly—hereditarily from my Grandpa or Great Aunt Bea? Or have I simply struck out and lost a random genetic lottery?

(In my family there are indeed traces of mental illness. No need to name names or dust off the family photo albums, but yes, if you climbed up my family tree you would find some depression and dementia instead of a bird's nest or bananas.)

A. "Studies at Stanford University that explored the genetic connection of bipolar disorder found that children with one biological parent with bipolar I or bipolar II disorder have an increased likelihood of getting bipolar disorder. In this study, researchers reported that 51 percent of the bipolar offspring had a psychiatric disorder, most commonly major depression, dysthymia (low-grade, chronic depression), bipolar disorder, or attention deficit hyperactivity disorder (ADHD)." *

*www.webmd.com/bipolar-disorder/guide/bipolar-disorder-causes?page=2)

Q. Nature versus nurture? Can bipolar disorder be brought on by our environments and experiences? Triggered by traumatic events or stressful situations—whether it's abuse, an abnormal childhood, bullying, or a bad break-up?

A. "Along with a genetic link to bipolar disorder, research shows that children of bipolar parents are often surrounded by significant environmental stressors. This may include living with a parent who has a tendency toward mood swings, alcohol or substance abuse, financial and sexual indiscretions, and hospitalizations. Environmental stressors also play a role in triggering bipolar episodes in those who are genetically predisposed. For example, children growing up in bipolar families may live with a parent who lacks control of moods or emotions. Some children may live with constant verbal or even physical abuse if the bipolar parent is not medicated or is using alcohol or drugs." *

*www.nami.org/Learn-More/Mental-Health-Conditions/Bipolar-Disorder

"... It has been known for some time that genetic history is a risk factor in the development and expression of bipolar disorder, yet there has been very little concrete information published on the specific genes involved. This information, together with a fuller understanding of other risk factors, which include stress, substance abuse and life circumstances, will help clinicians to understand the condition more fully, and to treat it more effectively. Much work is required in this respect." *

*www.elementsbehavioralhealth.com/
featured/breakthrough-in-the-search-for-bipolar-disorder-gene/

Clear as mud. My head hurts. I'm not sure about you, but I'm still confused. So many questions and not enough concrete answers. It's not black and white—there is no gene to test for or blood test to take. Out of millions of diagnoses, no two are alike; onset signs and symptoms are as unique as each person. And one need look no further than the plethora of treatment options to know that there isn't one specific pill that offers an instant fix for all. What works best for Rhonda up the road is guaranteed to be different from what helps Wayne down the lane—as different as their fashion sense and favourite foods.

We all have different stories—hurts, heartaches, successes, failures, and fears—that have contributed to who we are, what we do, and why. Reflecting on our life experiences can shed light and offer explanations. It's just as important to ask, "What *happened*?" instead of just, "What's wrong?"

And, what about me? I thought you'd never ask. I guess it's *that* time; time to put me under the microscope. Let's take a closer look, dissect, and discover what's happened in my life up until now.

"What's wrong?"
"What *happened*?"

You don't get a **second** chance
to make a first impression.

-Unknown

(*no pressure*)

An Awkward Introduction

"Nice to meet you. I'm mentally ill, *but* medicated. And by the way, my name is Julie." Can you imagine kicking off a job interview with that fully-loaded introduction? Never. Not in a million years. Disclosing a mental illness isn't the first (or fiftieth) thing I would ever do in a meet-and-greet. Nor would I recommend mentioning irritable bowel syndrome on a blind date. In my mind, those are both small parts of any person's pie—mere slivers—and certainly not the pieces to be served up first.

If you're lunching with a coworker who's got high cholesterol, hopefully their fatty food intake isn't the first, or last, topic of conversation. By the same token, if I spend the day with a friend, I hope they haven't braced themselves beforehand, wondering if I'm "running off the rails." I pray they are planning to meet with *me*, not my disorder, regardless of my mood—happy, sad, angry, or over-the-moon. In my opinion, all of these emotions are the result of being *human*, not of "being" *bipolar*.

Despite the first (or fiftieth, of course) impressions I might give, I am more than assaults the eye and ear; more than my bleached-blonde hair, haphazard behaviour, and high-pitched commentary. My waters run deep and thoughts many, but rarely do I trust others enough to let them dive into my world. However, it would appear as if today is *your* lucky day. So, without further ado, let's take the plunge (pun absolutely intended) and reintroduce ourselves. "Hi, my name is Julie..."

Some might call me a misfit—dramatic, passionate, quirky, eccentric, a square peg living in a world full of round holes. I would have to agree. That's definitely me. I *am* that gal who has unknowingly walked, at full speed, into men's washrooms and then emerged trailing toilet paper from my soles, *both* of them. I'm also the person who's poured coffee into my breakfast cereal without a second thought—a surefire way to improve the efficiency of my morning routine by taking me from half-asleep to wide-awake before the last spoonful. And this is assuming, of course, that the coffee pot was parked in its proper percolating spot in the first place. On the many days it wasn't, puddles of coffee pooled on the counter and flowed to the floor, giving my cabinets an instant antiqued look.

If you're going to be weird, be *confident* about it.

-Unknown

My mind is usually eighteen steps ahead of the already record-breaking speeds of my body parts, leading to uncoordinated mishaps wherever I go. I am constantly unhooking my snagged sweaters and stretched-out purse straps from door handles around town. While dining in restaurants, I've often mentally left the establishment and embarked on my next mission before even ordering my meal. Speaking of eating, despite my mouth being lion-sized and a dentist's dream, food may or may not make it inside due to my continuous gum-flapping. I can always count on a few spoonfuls of grub landing in the folds of my neck, scarf, or at the bottom of my purse. Drinking is just as difficult. My lips often fall a few feet short of connecting with the rim of my coffee cup—enough of a distance to make all the difference, and send coffee cascading down the front of my sure-to-be white silk shirt.

Now, when it comes to me operating any amount of wheels, it's a very dangerous undertaking. As a tween, a casual summer bike ride nearly turned deadly as I flew into a friend's driveway and slammed on the brake. That's right, the brake, *singular*, as in only *one* of two. Unfortunately for me, it was the front one. The next thing I remember is flying over the handle bars, flipping through the air, and landing in a crumpled heap on the ground. My unintentional stunt was undoubtedly quite the sight to see. To this day, my friend is baffled by my ability to bounce back, brush myself off, and follow her inside for some banana bread.

In later years, I learned to drive and often borrowed my parents' car. It wasn't a Rolls Royce, but it was reliable, always taking our family from point A to point B and back. That is, until the day it suspiciously needed a major mechanical overhaul. Seemingly out of the blue, the family car went from being in perfect working order to having a trashed transmission. Overnight. For months afterward, my dad shook his head and asked if I had any inkling as to why the car had suddenly let us down. I knew *exactly* why. I was sitting on a secret, but nothing could have broken my silence and made me confess. Until now.

I had been driving a few days before, cruising down the street at a good clip, and decided to change lanes. Unfortunately, on that day, my neck muscles proved to have a direct connection to my appendages; as I swivelled my head to shoulder check, my arm raised upward at high speed, making me an enthusiastic member of a marching band instead of a motorist. On its way up, my limb collided with the gear shift, taking the vehicle from Drive to Park in a instant. From full speed to fully stopped in seconds. And there I sat in the center lane, wide-eyed and whiplashed, wondering what the heck had happened and unsure of what to do next. Adding insult to my neck injury, a symphony of honks soon serenaded me. Unbelievably, I was able to hit the gas and head home, completely unaware of the irreversible damage I had just caused under the hood. (Dad, forgive me.)

Over the years, parking a vehicle has proven just as challenging. I've often made a spectacle of myself trying to parallel park in 20-foot spaces, breaking into a feverish sweat from the steering wheel workout and added pressure of amused onlookers. The scene has always ended with me abandoning my efforts and then circling the block for days in hopes of finding a cruise ship-sized opening to glide into bow first.

But have I always danced to the beat of a different drum? What kinds of impressions did I make as a small child—in the schoolyard, the neighbourhood, and my own shag-carpeted living room? Let's go back a few decades and find out.

1978

growing up

A Little Girl and a Lot of Chaos

Looking back at my early years, were there any signs or symptoms of what was to come? In hindsight, there were many. Some were even noticed, but only for what they seemed on the surface. In the 1980s the terms *manic depressive* and *bipolar* were rarely heard outside the walls of mental institutions. They were diagnoses used for adults, not for kids who threw temper tantrums or showed wild creativity in the classroom.

My mom recently told me I was always a bit of a brat—strong-willed, spirited, a "hot-headed handful," and *by far* the most difficult to raise of her four children. (Thanks, Mom.) Even as a little girl, I was out of control, yet cunningly in control at the same time. I often executed the most impressive games of Hide and Seek, just minutes before doctors' appointments I had no intention of attending. Sometimes I would wedge myself into the six-inch opening between our floral sofa and pea soup-coloured carpet. And other times, I'd claw my way to the tops of neighbours' trees. It worked. After frantic and unfruitful searches, my mom would be forced to admit defeat and reschedule my medical meetings.

The chaos that surrounded me spread far beyond the walls of my home and branches of nearby trees. On one occasion, I allowed a stick of bubble gum to cause quite a scene and ruin an entire school day.

Chewing on anything in my first-grade classroom, other than the tip of a pencil, was strictly forbidden for fear it would land on the newly installed (pea soup-coloured, of course) carpet. Regardless of the rule, in a daring act of youthful rebellion, I popped a piece of gum into my mouth. A few hours and a spelling test later, as I stood in line for the pencil sharpener, the stale and sticky substance leaped out of my mouth and onto the floor. Horrified, my first instinct was to cover it up, at full force, with my foot. There was no doubt the wad had been instantly embedded, was incapable of being extracted, and needed to be hidden at all cost. Dumbfounded, my teacher begged me to take my seat. Her efforts were in vain. It soon became clear I was prepared to stand in that spot for the rest of my life. The situation escalated; I soon found the principal glaring down at me, pleading for an explanation of my schoolroom standoff. In a last-ditch attempt to make me move, my mother was summoned. With a pregnant belly in front and my baby sister lagging behind, she walked a mile to the school (uphill, barefoot, in the snow), and issued me an ultimatum. It worked. My punishment? I can't remember, so it must have been minimal. My peculiar behaviour had likely left everyone at a loss for words *and* disciplinary action.

By the time I turned eight, my teachers were bolting up and taking notice—I was definitely different, always thinking outside the box, and running circles around my classmates in the academic department. Much to my delight, appropriate measures were taken to keep my mind stretched—I was shipped off to do two-week stints at a nearby school for whiz kids. We sang songs in foreign languages, wrote novels, and completed assignments suited for White House interns. I loved every minute of it—the creative freedom and confidence it gave me.

I would always return to "normal" life energized to change the world.

I created newspapers, drama productions, and student councils; crowning myself as chief editor, lead actress, and president, *before* auditions had been held or votes even cast. It was no surprise that I found myself at the mercy of my friends' jealousies. They gave me the evil eye and called me names—"Teacher's Pet" and "Smarty Pants." But all the while, I heard them saying something else. Their insults all screamed that they, too, wanted to be given child-prodigy status, an educational holiday, and some added attention.

The Big City and Some Fraud

As my teen years approached, raging hormones began to wreak havoc on my physical appearance and emotional stability. To add insult to injury, without warning, my parents pulled the rug out from under me and moved our family to the other side of the country. I was uprooted from the safety of a small town and planted in the heart of the big city, stolen far from friends and all familiarity. I was suddenly the new kid in town and in the schoolyard, recognized for my inability to "fit in" instead of my academic achievements. Feeling awkward and out of place, I withdrew and lost *all* confidence; instead of living outside the box, I crawled deep inside.

My wardrobe didn't help. With my family's every last dime having been spent on buying a house, there was nothing left over for brand new clothes, let alone any from the local secondhand store. I knew my chances of gaining popularity with my peers, dressed in outdated duds, were slim to none. Desperate times called for desperate measures. I decided to take matters into my own hands by transforming a pair of cheap, knock-off sport shoes into designer footwear—all it took was a piece of paper, some coloured pencils, and a little artistic talent. In an unbelievably bold and fraudulent move, I sketched a far more desirable brand label, cut it to size, and glued it on top of the no-name one.To this day, I'm not sure if anyone noticed my shoe-status upgrade or the fact that it was a phony one, but I sure felt better about myself for a moment. That is, until it started to rain at recess. In an instant, my hopes of being catapulted into the cool crowd were washed away.

Desperately trying to rebuild my reputation and reignite the fire she'd once seen within her little girl, my mom enrolled me in an academically advanced program and hoped for the best. It didn't work. Unfortunately, instead of giving me a creative outlet and confidence, it overloaded me with hours of extra homework. I dropped out.

But little did I know, my fake footwear and lack of follow-through would soon prove to be the very least of my worries; they were only the tip of what would soon become a tumultuous teenage iceberg.

"Feeling awkward and out of place,
I withdrew and lost *all* confidence;
instead of living outside the box,
I crawled deep inside."

1987

A Monobrow and a First Marriage

To describe my high school years as just an awkward phase would be a *gross* understatement. With no older sisters to steer me, I navigated most of my teen years without a map, confidence, or boyfriend. I never seemed to be as cool as my classmates, in any way. Even my hair fell flat before first class. Despite hours of backcombing and emptying fifty cans of extra-hold hairspray, my coif never seemed to poof up as high as my friends'.

My body was just as disappointing. Instead of prompting my breasts to develop, puberty placed an order for my eyebrows to fuse together. Unfortunately, it didn't take long for my classmates to notice. By senior year, my fan base consisted of a gang of boys, spurred on by each other as they teased and hurled insults my way. I was greeted each and every morning with an invasion of my personal space and a game of cruel charades. As they motioned the actions of shaving, with buzzing sounds for added effect, it took only seconds for me to clue in and guess correctly. Mortified, I would run to the nearest washroom stall and bawl, but I always tried my best to pull myself together and put on a brave face before the starting bell. On one occasion, my opponents seized the opportunity to steal my textbooks and add artistic embellishments to all the female faces inside. With the help of a few permanent markers, the women had become more masculine, magically growing monobrows to match mine.

But despite those bullies, when it came to the male species, I remained a hopeless romantic. Some might even say I was extremely awkward, borderline obsessive, and at times, downright creepy. I *always* had a crush on some unsuspecting guy and it *always* went unrequited. My designated spot was on the sidelines at school dances. That is, until I turned sweet sixteen. Finally, after years of practicing my kissing techniques on pillows and plush toys, I got the chance to put my training to the test. It was a feeble, flustered attempt; a sloppy, slobbery smooch that never would have made it into the movies. My not-so-smooth moves were mocked and made fun of, but it didn't matter; I had finally kissed a living, breathing boy.

Remarkably, despite being teased about my eyebrow (singular, as in only *one* of what should have been *two*) and the way I locked lips, I still welcomed any type of attention that came my way. Unfortunately, it was almost always negative. I soon realized I could get further with my peers by playing the "kooky" card; by being the weird and goofy one, the girl who was much easier to make fun of than invite to a party or onto the dance floor. It suited me just fine. I wouldn't have known how to behave in the cool crowd or on the dance floor anyway. I continuously convinced myself that if I did dare accept such invites, I'd be the only sober soul in the place, completely out of sync, and single.

My prom night proved all my insecure assumptions correct. On that celebratory night, my date was a boy, and a friend, nothing more. And by the end of the evening, *much less*. Finding him in the bushes with another girl was probably the biggest reason why. Suffice it to say, my seductive tactics for the night had backfired.

My original plan was to silently seduce the boys by slipping into a hand-sewn, sexy, and rather "revealing" black dress. I purchased a pattern and some fabric, but no amount of money could have bought me the confidence to wear it. With only a few weeks to spare, I chickened out and opted for plan B. Well, that "B" could have easily been an abbreviation for "bridal;" my backup frock was snow-white and only a few ruffles shy of a full-blown wedding gown. To this day, I am shocked that my date willingly posed for photos, knowing that they could easily be passed off as proof of a first marriage.

Even still, I held out hope that the guys would look my way; that out of a sea of sexy girls, they would choose the "fish out of water," the gal who screamed innocent, inexperienced, and "I do." I couldn't have been more wrong. There I sat, at the end of the night, alone on the sidewalk, as my fellow graduates stumbled around and spilled their drinks *on me*. Once again, desperate times, called for desperate measures. In a final attempt to fit in, I grabbed a bottle of booze and dashed into a nearby bathroom. To ensure I held true to my strict religious upbringing, I dumped the contents, gave the bottle a thorough rinse, and filled it to the brim with water. For the rest of the night, I kept my drink close and fingers crossed, praying I wouldn't be found out as a fraud.

But despite my many failed attempts and embarrassing moments, my pursuit of romance (and the male species) continued at full throttle. No amount of rejection—none, whatsoever—seemed to slow me down or break my stride.

Sometimes we create
our own heartbreaks
through *expectation*.

-Unknown

A Few Men and a Missed Memo

Even the most carefully laid plans fall apart and I was living proof. I had made arrangements to move away and attend school, all because of a boy. He wasn't my boyfriend, or even a friend-friend, just a guy I'd met for a minute and fallen madly "in lust" with. And despite him living thousands of miles away, I was convinced we were only a few dates and a cross-country move away from getting married, taking out a mortgage, and making babies. I wasted no time applying to a university just steps from his front door. It worked. An acceptance letter made its way into my mailbox. But within seconds of getting the green light for my grand scheme, I made a devastating discovery—my future husband had apparently missed the memo about our fairy tale future. Not only had he enrolled in a different school, it was a million miles away.

Unable to back out of my plans, I wallowed in self-pity and found a local boy to temporarily ease my pain. He was the quintessential bad boy—he smoked, drank more than a drop, and dabbled in drugs. I fell fast and hard. Much to my dismay, the day eventually came for me to follow through on the plans I had made months before. It was time to bid my boyfriend farewell. We promised our undying love to each other at the airport gate and committed to a long distance love affair. But before the wheels of my plane had even lifted from the runway, *everything* changed. Within days, late-night phone calls and lovey-dovey conversations dwindled. I was lonely, homesick, and so very sad; instead of helping to ease the pain and stress of moving away, my so-called boyfriend was causing even more. It wasn't long before my calls went unanswered altogether and my overactive and inventive mind went into overdrive. Every possible scenario went through my mind: Had he been hurt? Jailed? Killed? Abducted by aliens? Even more devastating, had his heart been stolen away or willingly given to someone else? Whatever his reasons, he made the callous and cold-hearted decision to drop off the radar. I spent sleepless nights worrying and internalized everything. My heart broke.

Finally, after what seemed like an eternity, he called. But it wasn't with news I was hoping to hear—he had shacked up with an old flame, a gal pal whom he defended as "just a friend," allegedly "without benefits." Filled with paranoia and suspicion, I placed a midnight call to scope out the situation and stake my claim. His new roommate picked up. Trying my best to disguise my disgust, I asked to speak with my man. Unfortunately, it took less time than it ever should have for his voice to come on the line—the phone had been passed over in seconds and was glaring proof that the rent bill and kitchen pantry weren't the only things he and his ex were sharing. I finally put the pieces together and pulled the wool from my eyes. I. Was. Devastated.

Even so, I held on to the hope that our relationship could somehow be saved. I waited for his call. It never came. A month went by in s-l-o-w motion. With each passing second, minute, day, I sank deeper into a dark pit of depression. I was humiliated and hurt. Never in a million years did I think he would cut ties in such a cowardly way—with silence. I had been in love and it had left, without warning or even a proper farewell.

Finally, I mustered up enough courage and self-respect to end things, the only way I knew how—with a letter. It was one of the most gut-wrenching decisions of my life. I knew my one-way piece of mail meant saying goodbye to what I thought we had, and all my hopes that it could have been so much more. Clutching my envelope, I sobbed in the corner of the local post office for what seemed like an eternity before finding the strength to purchase its postage—much higher-priced, to guarantee its delivery by demanding a signature at the door. Dramatic? Very. I looked away, unable to watch as my letter, and future, vanished into the slot behind the counter. It was over. I slid the tracking number into my wallet, walked home, wailed, and waited. I was certain I would hear something. *Anything.* That eventually there would be a desperate call to show that I mattered, that we mattered, or even to say "I'm sorry," so that at the very least I could move on without a mile-long list of unanswered questions. I needed closure. But still, only silence.

My anxiety levels reached all-time highs during the months that followed. I often found myself incapacitated on campus, unable to leave my dormitory and washroom stalls; I was convinced that others were waiting on the other side to watch, judge, and laugh at me. I feared they would label me an imposter, someone who had no place pursuing an education or an eventual career out in the real world. I skipped meals and most of my classes, but somehow pushed through. Despite my struggles, I fostered friendships, wrote essays on books I'd never read, took tests without studying, and most important, didn't fail. But although I passed my courses, it didn't mean I could keep it up and continue.

After only one year away, I returned home empty-handed—without good grades or a soul mate. I was miserable. In my mind, moving back in with mommy and daddy and enrolling in a local college were both considered booby prizes. My depression and anxiety remained.

But no matter how rough the storm, how dark the skies, clouds eventually roll away and blue skies emerge. The sun is always there. And sometimes, sunshine comes in the form of someone who strolls into our lives at the most unexpected and much-needed moment.

1995

married life

Fate And Finding A Mate
from this day forward and a few steps backward

I had only been home from university mere minutes, sulking in my sweats and inhaling truckloads of chocolate, when fate smiled my way. In a seemingly random encounter, I ran into an old friend (the boy kind) I'd met a year earlier through a mutual acquaintance. He had originally been introduced as my perfect match, a surefire soul mate, someone with whom I even shared a strict religious upbringing. "You two would be perfect together, get married, and live happily ever after."

Our matchmaking friend was right. I liked this new guy. A lot. He was witty, kind, strappingly good looking, with a big heart *and* shoe size—all the attributes I'd scribbled down on my "knight in shining armour" list as a daydreaming teen. But the timing hadn't been right until that fateful afternoon when sparks were relit and flew wildly about.

"I really like you and would love the chance to date you. Call me if you feel the same," he said with a smile. His approach was confident, straightforward, rather business-like, and it worked. I dialed his digits before bedtime and, as they say in the movies, "the rest is history." He had caught me without a chase.

It was a whirlwind romance. We were inseparable. Bridal magazines soon became a regular part of our dinner dates and, shockingly, he didn't make a mad dash for the door at the sight of white gowns and reception ideas. It worked. A diamond engagement ring soon wiggled its way onto my finger, and a wedding date was set. At record speed, seven months to be exact, we found ourselves standing at the altar of a quaint country chapel, pledging our undying "I do's."

But had I fooled him? Kept my mask from cracking? Had I flashed any neon signs of my rollercoaster existence, explosive emotions, or the possibility of an impending mental illness? Yes, I *absolutely* did. There were many red flags. They were *all* noticed, but most were seen as attention-seeking, situational, and solvable. The rest were passed off as PMS, a bad hair day, or the fault of a full moon. Having my new husband stick by my side led me to believe there would always be a free pass (or fifty) that would allow me to get away with just about anything.

"Why didn't you run for the hills when you had the chance?" I've often asked in the twenty years that have followed. His reply has always remained the same: "I loved you with all my heart and thought it would only take a few hugs and some added care to keep you happy. I also knew if I married you, life would always be exciting." He couldn't have been more right on that last prediction, but as far as only needing a little extra loving, it would soon prove nowhere near enough. A cuddle and some encouraging words would not be enough to help me conquer my fears, tame my mind, or balance the chemical makeup of my brain. It would take more. *So much more.*

"I never felt as if I was
actually living, in the moment
or in first person.
Racing thoughts and endless worries
had stolen me far from the front row
of my *very own* life."

A Worried Wife And A Young Mom

My husband and I dove into married life head-first from the high diving board and made quite the splash. By our second anniversary, a tempting job offer had come my husband's way. He accepted it. We soon moved to Seattle and... made a *baby*. That's right, I could barely operate a car with confidence, but had a newborn to care for; one that demanded all my time and energy. My days were spent alone in a dark apartment washing dishes, changing diapers, and daydreaming. If I did dare venture out, I never went far; having no car, friends, or spending money kept me close to home. Even so, I never complained or caused a fuss. After all, driving had always been something that sent me over the edge.

It wasn't long before my husband's hard work paid off and a promotion came his way. But although his climbing the corporate ladder would put more money in the bank, it would also give us less time together; long days in the office and extended business trips became the new norm.

My hubby needed a ride to the airport, and I needed a tranquilizer. Anticipating the driving I would need to do—shoulder checks, lane changes, and sixty-point turns—threw me into a state of panic for days beforehand. On the morning of, I mustered up every ounce of courage within me and gave myself a pep talk. It was very short-lived. The moment my husband said his goodbyes at the airport door, my confidence vanished. No sooner had I hopped over into the driver's seat and pulled away from the curb, than fear set in and tears welled up. Shaking, I wrapped my fingers around the wheel in a death grip and started sobbing. I envisioned the very worst—side-swiping a cement barricade, careening into oncoming traffic, and causing a five-hundred car pile-up, with casualties. Yes, I would most definitely be headlining the six o'clock news that night. And so there I was, having a full-blown panic attack at fifty miles an hour, with no one but a newborn baby to talk me down or take the wheel. The ironic thing was, with the exception of that "marching band" mishap and my pathetic parallel parking skills, I was a law-abiding citizen with a spotless driving record who, even to this day, insists on using turn signals on curvy roads and in abandoned parking lots (safety first). No, I'd never needed to flirt or flash my non-existent cleavage in attempts to avoid speeding tickets. Eventually, I reached home. It took me days to recover, before once again having to face my fears and fetch my husband upon his return.

Before the year was over, we were on the move again. Another exciting career change was launching my husband into the dot-com world of technical geeks and millionaire-making IPOs. We crammed all our earthly belongings into the back seat of our car and relocated to the Golden State of California. Knowing I would be living in the land of palm trees and eternal blue skies made me more excited than a kid on Christmas morning. And despite us having only four dollars (and wheels) to our name, this was our big break. *My* big break. I now had the chance to start a new life. But the billion dollar question was, could I be brave enough to step outside my front door and do it? I was sure going to try.

It was my daughter and me against the world. We spent our days watching cartoons and making crafts. She was always my go-to excuse to hide from the outside world. If we stayed in isolation, I wouldn't have to answer phone calls, set boundaries, attend mommy groups, or arrange play dates. This self-imposed solitary confinement suited me just fine.

Despite my best efforts to avoid the human race, I ran out of places to run. Sunday mornings were no exception. It was impossible to attend church without someone offering a warm welcome and an invitation to dinner. As a preacher's daughter, it was a social scene I should have been more than comfortable with. To the contrary, every person and invite that came my way set off alarm bells and brought the urge to find the nearest emergency exit. I'm getting back behind the wheel now, brace yourself.

I soon realized that if I ever wanted to escape the "prison" I'd locked myself in, I would need to break out from behind bars and get behind the wheel. And so, that's exactly what I did. It worked. The more I drove, the more comfortable I became. I would feel an overwhelming sense of accomplishment on those days, as if I could take on the world or at least drive all over it.

However, there were still daily activities that made my blood pressure soar. At the top of my list? Filling my car with fuel. I secretly wished the gas tank would always stay full, so I'd never need a fill-up. But eventually, the gauge would plummet toward empty and I'd have to face my refuelling fears. Would I have to wait in line, and for how long? What if another car arrived at the same time? Would I pull up close enough for the hose to reach? But my biggest fear by far? A defective nozzle splashing gas in every direction—into my eyes, mouth, hair, and soaking my sure-to-be white silk shirt. Such a scene would surely end with a wet t-shirt contest, emergency eye rinse, and an ambulance.

I apologize, profusely. The previous list is exhausting to read. And unbelievably, or believably, it's only a small sampling of the worries that would be racing through my mind during any given gas-up.

My brain has too many tabs
open.

-Unknown

Every day was *such* a struggle. From the minute I woke until the moment I fell asleep, anything and everything I could worry about, I did. It would start with something as simple as getting ready for the day; stepping into the shower and putting on my makeup stressed me beyond belief. Would I be able to fully rinse my shampoo or properly blend my blush? It all overwhelmed me. I never felt as if I was actually living, in the moment or in first person. Racing thoughts and endless worries had stolen me far from the front row of my *very own* life. By the end of each day, it was all I could do to lay my head on my pillow and hope for a few hours of sleep so I could "rise and repeat" the next day.

Please forgive me
if I don't talk much at times,
it's loud enough in *my head.*

-Unknown

comic relief

A Full-Priced Fuel-Up

Hell had frozen over. It was a rare occasion; I was going to open my front door, step over the threshold, and leave my apartment. Yes, I had made plans to be somewhere other than plopped on my sofa with a bowl of popcorn and a pile of trashy magazines. Making the day happen entailed an early morning drop-off of my husband at the "salt mines" so I could retain custody of the family car. After giving him a parting peck (sloppy and slobbery, of course), I hopped in the driver's seat and started on my way. Everything was going according to plan and despite the gas gauge heading into the red, I was confident I wouldn't need to stop for a fill-up before sunset. Now, if *you* read your books in chronological order, you'll remember that "gassing up" was always a source of extreme angst.

As I cruised by the local gas station, I noticed a hub of activity; quite the commotion—balloons, music, the six o'clock news team, and a long lineup of cars. The curious cat in me temporarily overrode my refuelling fears. I pulled a u-turn (a legal one, you can be sure) to find out what all the fuss was about.

It was a once-in-a-lifetime deal on fuel: Regular grade petrol priced far below market value. The wait would be long, but worth it, so I secured my spot in line—car number eighty-seven. Finally my turn came. I pulled up to the pump, hit my fuel choice, and started to fill up. Out of the corner of my eye, I could see cameras rolling as a fellow fueller was being interviewed. I hoped I would be next; that is, until I made a startling and humiliating realization—only Regular was on sale. I had selected Premium. Unknowingly, I'd been ecstatically filling my tank with full-priced fuel. Completely unaware that I could have easily hung up the nozzle, re-selected the blow-out price, and saved a fortune, I continued to let the liquid gold flow and hoped no one would notice. I was terrified of a reporter coming my way and finding me out as the biggest ditz on the planet—someone willing to wait two hours to pay top dollar. I felt like an absolute idiot—stupid and pathetic—for being incapable of cashing in on the deal of the century.

Later on, I called my husband to recount my gas station blunder and confess that I'd blown the budget. Although he did offer his understanding, I'm almost certain I could hear his howls of laughter long after I'd hung up.

Unfortunately, my hubby didn't always find my actions amusing or offer forgiveness so easily.

Integrity is doing the right thing when *no one* is looking.

-Unknown

Dirty Laundry and Dishonesty

Dirty laundry has always piled up and overwhelmed me. The more kids I birthed, the bigger the backlog became, and the more water I wasted rewashing loads that had been left damp for days. My inability to clean our clothes always impacted my husband the most. As a white-collared professional, his threads needed to be fresh and pressed at all times; it was never an option for him to pass by the water cooler wearing a stained shirt or crinkled khakis. However, when it came to his undergarments, it was an entirely different story.

My husband's underwear drawer should have been impossible to push in; I had purposely purchased him hundreds of pairs to ensure he would always have clean ones. In hindsight, I should have bought even more.

"Hey honey, do I have any clean underwear? My drawer's empty."

"Yup, sure thing, no problem, coming right up!" I cheerily hollered as I crapped my pants, trying to disguise the sheer panic his words had induced. I flew down a flight of stairs and into the laundry room to scour for a clean pair. Fully aware that I'd opted to "play" that week—bargain hunt and paint a few canvases (and my toenails)—instead of wash his clothes, I prayed for a miracle. It never came. That left me with only two options. The first was to simultaneously blow-dry and iron a sopping wet pair, in hopes of taking them from dripping to dry before he slid them on. Plan B was much more daring—it was dirty, disgusting, and downright deceitful. *I opted for it.* Springing into action, I sifted through the soiled clothes and found the most convincingly "clean" pair. I tossed them in the dryer for some heat before polishing them off, literally, with a sheet of heavily scented fabric softener.

"I'm out of the tub, did you find a clean pair?" my hubby groggily asked.

"Oh, you bet I did babe, on my way!"

Despite the benefit of him being half-asleep, I still wasn't sure if I could dupe him. Doing my best to cover up a sly smirk, I passed over his warmed, folded undies and avoided all eye contact. The only things missing from my suspicious hand delivery were Belgian chocolates, a bottle of champagne, and some background music. My usually trusting husband looked deep into my eyes, slowly smelled his undergarment, and a rat. Once again, I had raised red flags and he had noticed *all* of them.

The interrogation began. "Why are you acting so nervous? Are these clean? Would you dare pass me a dirty pair?" Yes, I would, and yes, I did. My gig was up. I burst into laughter. There was nothing left for me to do but slither away with a mixture of guilt and remorse running through my veins. I had broken my husband's trust. To this day, I'm still working on regaining it; any underwear that magically appears out of thin air is instantly met with skepticism. I must shamefully admit that since then, I've successfully deceived him three more times, been caught once, and sent him off to work "commando" more times than he'd ever admit around the water cooler.

It's time to stop this deceitful, dirty, knicker-talk and switch to a more respectable topic. I'm going to dig *deep*, find my manners, and prove I wasn't raised in a barn or by a pack of wolves. I'll write about something more prim and proper, something more refined... how about something related to royalty?

"Plan B was much more daring–
it was dirty, disgusting,
and downright deceitful.
I opted for it."

Off to Visit the Queen
turn down the baby and crank up the volume

I was finally taking advantage of the fact that my husband travelled to Britain on business. With an overstuffed suitcase and freshly plucked brows, I was flying across the pond to meet him. Not only would I be able to confirm that it was his work, not a young English "rose," that lured him abroad each month, I'd be fulfilling a lifelong dream of exploring England—the Cotswolds, Covent Garden, Union Jacks and Big Ben. And I was even going to try my luck at looking the "right" way when I crossed the street.

The plane was filling with passengers from every direction. People and their carry-ons were crowding me and inducing claustrophobia. After triple-checking my boarding pass and feeling confident I had found my proper seat, I plopped myself in place. So there I sat, smack dab in the middle of the centre row. I knew it was only a matter of minutes before I'd be "sandwiched in" for a sleepless night. I watched and waited for my seatmates to show up. As each handsome businessman walked by, I breathed a gust of relief—the mere thought of spending the evening beside a man who wasn't my husband sent me spinning. I would surely find myself checking if I'd slathered on enough "pit stick," hyperventilating, and then grasping for the oxygen mask above me. With fingers (and toes) crossed, I hoped for the best—a mime, a painfully shy teen, a blow-up

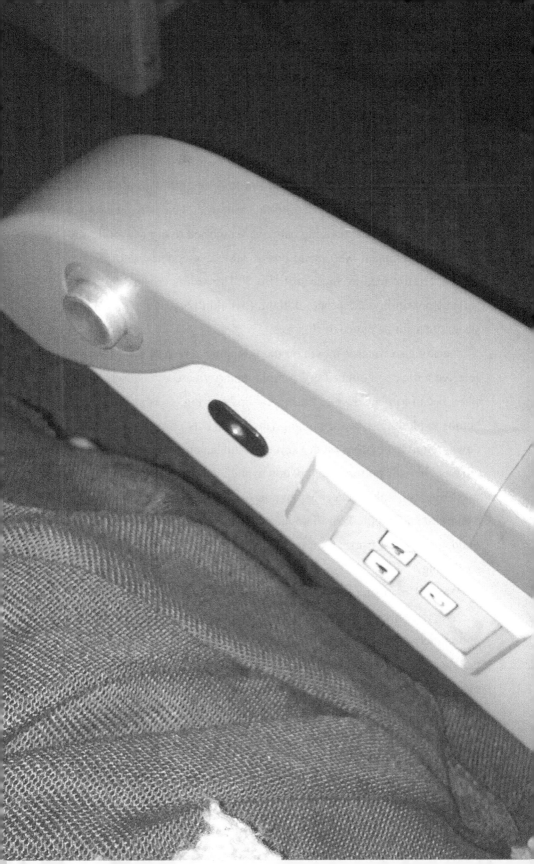

doll, or even a debarked beagle—I just needed anyone or anything that would up my chances of an uneventful evening. Much to my surprise, as the surrounding seats were claimed, the ones beside me remained empty. A few more passengers and minutes passed. I was thrilled at the thought of being on my own, able to stretch out and snuggle with a few extra paper-thin "blankets" and lice-infested pillows. Then it happened... a young couple with a screaming baby were escorted to my row, followed by a flight attendant who made unavoidable eye-contact with me and asked, "Excuse me, are these seats free?" Her words crushed my spirit and any possibility of a peaceful flight. I wouldn't be catching a wink of sleep; not a single ounce of shut-eye.

Deciding to watch a movie on the miniature screen in front of me, I selected a flick and donned my complimentary five-cent headset. As the show began to play, despite the actors' lips moving, guns shooting, and bombs exploding, I heard nothing (insert crickets chirping). I reached down, found the buttons on my arm rest, and began pressing wildly—the top one, then the bottom one, up, down, and all around, a thousand times over. But still, only silence. My button pushing became more violent in a desperate attempt to hear dialogue and drown out that baby beside me. Suddenly, I felt a firm tap on my shoulder, "Miss, can I help you with something?"

"Nope, I'm great," I lied, as I continued to lip-read in front of me.

"Are you sure you don't need anything? You've been ringing the Call button incessantly for the last five minutes." He soon clued in to the fact that despite wearing my headphones and an intense action scene playing out on the screen in front of me, I could still hear his every word and answer his questions. "Perhaps, just maybe, you've been trying to adjust the volume?"

The mortified look on my face must have said it all and confirmed his suspicions. Unknowingly, I'd been serenading the cabin with a symphony of "dings." Yes, I was a bleached blonde heading abroad, and the entire plane now knew it. I just hoped I wasn't the first, or last, person who had missed the memo that planes in the twenty-first century had switched to a touch-screen system.

ding.

A Root Canal and a Rice Casserole

I have never *(never, ever, ever)* had an interest in cooking. In my mind, the preparation and consumption of food is a means of pure sustenance, not an art form or source of pleasure. My motto has always been, "slap something together and send it down the hatch," so I could move on to more important things. Besides, by the time dinner rolled around, my energy and creativity had long been spent. Putting supper on the table was a chore that carried the excitement level of a root canal. I tried to cut corners whenever and however I could—always pushing the limits of best-before dates and recycling rice from Friday night takeout into not-so-new casseroles throughout the following week.

And so, you can only imagine how dicey things got when folks from the outside world entered my home for a meal. Yes, others did accept my invitations to dinner, but always at their own risk.

It was the holidays and I was hosting special guests from out of town. The stakes were high and I needed to use every ounce of culinary skill within me to create a meal to remember. Spaghetti it was, with some added maple syrup and sausage in the straight-out-of-the-can sauce. After all, sometimes an extra ingredient or two can make all the difference... *all the difference in the world.*

A few hours later, as we sat digesting dinner, enjoying drinks, and devouring dessert, I was confident the evening had been a smashing success; that is, until one female partygoer suddenly made a mad dash to the loo. Several minutes and flushes later, she emerged looking whitewashed and much worse for wear. Over the next 48 hours every last one of us dropped like flies. We had all been poisoned. I prayed for a meat recall to get me off the hook. It never came. I had officially learned my lesson—best-before dates are more than mere suggestions. *So much more.*

Believably, it wasn't the first or last time things had gone sideways in the kitchen. You see, even if the main meal ended without incident, it didn't mean anyone was "out of the woods." I would always offer my guests coffee afterward. Much to my dismay, they always said yes. As soon as they uttered the words, "I'd love a cup," panic would set in. Would the brew be too strong, weak, or taste like stinky feet? And how the heck did they take it? Hot and blonde or beige and sweet? With just a pinch of sugar and millimeter of milk? I felt I could only successfully serve it "black." Introducing cream and sugar, always meant more ways for me to mess up; endless variations were all open to interpretation and always sent me into top-secret, taste-testing mode. Yes, it was a regular occurrence for me to sneak a sip, wipe my lipstick off the rim, and then serve it up with a smile. (Did I just admit that? Yes. Yes, I did.)

Gathering humans around my dinner table for a few hours was never difficult; however, when it came to people becoming a more permanent fixture in my life, it wasn't quite as easy.

2006

the life I was "living"

A Masked Woman

Good friends were hard to find, and even harder to keep. But I was blessed with a few people who made me feel safe enough to let my guard down, answer their knocks on my front door, and return their phone calls. Over time, they succeeded in coaxing me out of my shell, and my house.

I had accepted an invitation to attend a weekly mom's group at my local church. It involved a freeway drive and socializing with strangers, but I made the trek and enjoyed the gathering. I became a regular attendee. Before long, I was found out for my artistic talents and was asked to coordinate craft making. Again, I said yes. A few successful sponge-painting lessons later, a microphone was shoved into my hand and my body pushed onto a stage; I'd been given the opportunity to talk about more meaningful things than tie-dye shirts and glitter glue.

I loved sharing openly and honestly, but only from afar. Despite everyone's eyes being fixed on me, the stage was the safest place to be. Being a few feet higher and farther from the other moms made me feel protected; as long as I was up there, flapping my gums, no one could talk to me. But most important of all? In my insecure mind, my designated spot on stage validated my attendance at the event, residency in the state, legitimacy as a person, and yes, even my existence on the planet. Unfortunately, my talks would eventually end, and the instant they did, my safety bubble would burst. I became vulnerable, no longer buffered by an invisible wall that separated me from my audience and saved me from small talk.

My inability to say "no," set boundaries, and just be "me," made conversations and most situations seem life-threatening. I began to feel the crushing pressure of always obliging and keeping up my Oscar performance long after I'd stepped off any stage. Would people still like me if I couldn't? I sure didn't think so.

Don't get me wrong, I did have days when I was *genuinely* happy. I *could* be the "life of the party." If there was a karaoke machine nearby, be assured I'd be the first one to grab it and belt out a tune (totally off-key, of course). But those moments were very short-lived and certainly not the norm.

Unfortunately, it seemed whatever I did (or sang), people, shockingly, wanted more. But I was a "one-hit wonder," a "one-day wonder" at best, and could rarely deliver a second show, let alone an encore of even one song. Still, I couldn't bear the thought of disappointing my "fans." If I was a no-show or just sat solemnly on the sidelines, people would surely ask, "Where is the Julie we know and love? What's wrong? Are you okay?" And so, my act continued.

It was all my fault. I was caught in a vicious cycle that *I* had created and was continuing to fuel. It was never an option to have a down day in public. The only version of myself I let people see was the happy-go-lucky, karaoke-singing, joke-telling Julie. I gave no other reference point for my personality. It was an exhausting way to live and would soon prove impossible to sustain. Who could ever live their life with the same smile, at the same speed, day in and day out? Despite my best efforts, not me. Wearing a mask and projecting a false image was quickly taking its toll. I was cracking, imploding, exploding, and spewing all my pent up frustration and anger onto those closest to me. The ones I loved the very most always got my worst.

My "cruising altitude" was often higher than most people in the world, but my eventual descent always ended in an uncontrolled crash landing. Without warning, storm clouds rolled in. The sun disappeared and so did I.

"On my darkest days,
I would feel turned around...
...and upside down."

DEPRESSION

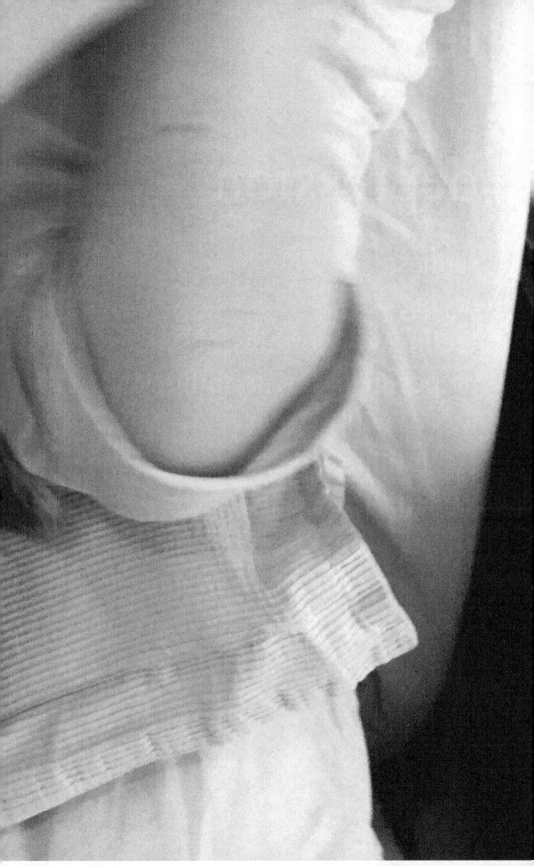

depression

sadness

crying

feelings of worthlessness

preoccupation with failures

loss of self-esteem

forgetfulness

difficulty concentrating

difficulty making decisions

misinterpretation of events

loss of interest in hobbies

lethargy
insomnia
social isolation
irritability and agitation
low energy
changes in appetite
oversleeping
decreased sexual drive
loss of pleasure
suicidal thoughts

"I'm doing awesome.
Thanks for asking."

"I couldn't be doing worse.
How dare you ask."

"Yes, I'd *love* to meet you for a latte."

"I'd rather have five root canals done
than meet you for even one sip of coffee."

"The simplest things became a struggle, the basics *unbearable*."

Granny Panties and Groceries

The best way to paint a true picture of my depressive episodes is with my words because, chances are, you would have never seen them firsthand. That's right, during my darkest hours, sightings were few and far between.

Looking back, on all those days when I couldn't muster up the energy to don my "mask" and face the world, I crawled into a cave. I hid the only way I knew how, the only place I could—behind a barricaded front door and closed curtains, with Airplane mode enabled and voicemail disabled. In the solitude and isolation of my home and mind I felt safe.

I also liked to be cozy and comfortable. *Very* cozy. *Too* comfortable. Much to my husband's horror, oversized and extremely unflattering clothes became the norm; lacy thongs and negligees were replaced with granny panties and penguin print pajamas. With my fire-starting eyeglasses crazy-glued to my face, I allowed my brows to fuse back together and my teeth to grow fuzz. Neglectful? Very.

Friends' desperate attempts to reach me were often unsuccessful; there was rarely anything they could do or say to evoke a response. The more they "chased," the faster I ran, and, more clever, a hiding spot I found. Giving me space, time, and no guilt trip were their only chances of convincing me to "come out and play."

Now, if hell froze over and I *did* make it out my front door, doing anything seemed more difficult than walking a tightrope across Manhattan, in stilettos, during a *snow storm*. The simplest things became a struggle, the basics unbearable—eating, walking, inhaling, exhaling (it actually *was* that bad). I would become acutely aware of every move I made and breath I took. Even strutting down the street posed problems as I staggered to-and-fro, zigzagging back and forth, overanalyzing every movement of my limbs. I'm convinced the police were only a few streets and strawberry-filled donuts away from showing up to administer a sobriety test.

Grocery shopping ranked high on my list of dreaded tasks. After all, a stroll down the breakfast food aisle could have turned disastrous on a dime—seeing a few folks standing by the Cheerios brought the fear of being asked about the sugar content of a certain cereal. Speaking of sugar, in cafés, I'd only have the confidence to order a plain coffee and choke it back "black," despite loving it as sweet as syrup with five inches of foam on top. Let's keep this list going, shall we? I would also speed past designer boutiques; you know, the kind that showcase one shoe per shelf, have supermodelesque staff, and security guards at the door? I felt so unworthy of setting foot in such high-end establishments and incapable of making eye contact with such "perfect" salespeople. Instead, I'd opt to browse in big box stores and thrift shops, where I could blend in and duck for cover in clothes racks if need be. (Self-check out, anyone? Yes, please.) Fading far into the background of *every* scene was the name of my game.

Having plans sounds like
a good idea *until*
you have to put clothes on
and leave your house.

-Unknown

Irrational Fears and Overreactions

Often, it's what I did (and at times, still do) best—overthink, obsess, catastrophize, jump to the *worst* possible conclusions, and then stay in that state of unrest far longer than I should. I would even worry if the neighbour's cousin's mother's brother's cat had fleas and was up to date on its immunizations. Hey, if you were hanging with me, there was never a reason for you to stress. You could sit back and relax because I had you (and the entire continent) covered. And so, you can only imagine how intense things got when it came to worrying about me, myself, and I.

I've always cared too much about what others think—of my decisions, actions, words, shade of lipstick, even the direction I part my hair and twirl my pasta. In the past, my most dysfunctional reactions came when emails went unanswered within the first few seconds. By minute two I was spiralling out of control. After five hours of not hearing back? I would be drenched in sweat, feverishly checking my inbox along with my blood pressure. Was it something I wrote or didn't write? Had my well-intentioned words been taken the wrong way, the right way, or some warped way in between? I would lie in bed each night and reread my messages, word-for-word, syllable-by-syllable, with every possible intonation. Could my, "Hope you're doing great!" have been interpreted as, "You are *such* a *loser,* your existence is *forgettable*; now there *is* a very *slim* chance that things *might* have taken a turn for the better, but I *highly* doubt it."? Or, had my, "Hope your summer plans are as exciting as mine?" morphed into, "You're *pathetic*, and if you hadn't realized it before now, my vacations are *far* superior to yours and *always* will be."? Sending follow-up clarifications and extensive apologies constantly crossed my mind. Never once did reason or rationality enter the equation. Nope, I never considered the possibility that people were busy living their lives—with high-powered jobs, kids to care for, vacations to take, dogs to walk, and cats to shampoo. And no, I never entertained the idea that, shockingly, I was not the centre of everyone's universe; that I wasn't the first thing to cross my friends' minds in the morning and their final thought before falling asleep.

Thank goodness, my fears were almost always proven unfounded. I would eventually receive replies within a week or six months, and my paranoia would be put to rest! I hadn't offended anyone!! There was usually an apology or half-decent reason for their tardy reply—a jam-packed schedule, a trip to the moon, being trapped in a full body cast, or having just come out of a coma! In a matter of only a few sentences, my confidence would come back and my spirits would soar. My entire world (and my mood) would be turned right side up in an instant!!!

MANIA

When she was down she was
very, very down,

but when she was high,
she could *fly*.

-Unknown

mania

silliness
periods of euphoria
restlessness
racing thoughts
excessive talking
misinterpretation of events
explosive creativity
excessive energy

extreme irritability
overspending
sense of grandiosity
narcissism
decreased need for sleep
increased sexual drive
poor judgment
recklessness

A Superhero and a Shirt Sale
Picasso and a Pulitzer Prize

Mania. It is a feeling like no other—incredible, amazing, exhilarating, intoxicating. Despite not having slept in days, I feel like Wonder Woman, flying fifty-five thousand feet above the clouds, let alone the ground. I don't think twice, or even once, about stopping, doing a 360-degree spin, and striking up a conversation with a stranger in the street. Strutting into a café and ordering a custom-made coffee under a fake foreign name (one at least fourteen letters long), is fun instead of feared. The sun shines and stars align, all just for me. Traffic lights turn vibrant green and police look the other way as I speed by without my hands on the wheel. Premium parking spaces open up, and if there's only one designer shirt left on the rack, it's in my size *and* on sale. The world is my oyster.

I am unstoppable, willing to try just about anything, and often with great success (cue Bryan Adams to pull me up on stage to "sing" with him). Did I really do that? Yes. Yes, I did. Instead of shoe labels, I'll wake before sunrise and knock off a Picasso painting before noon. And, of course, in my manic moments, I have wholeheartedly believed that this book will become a *New York Times* bestseller, help billions, and land me a Pulitzer Prize for my back pocket. Narcissistic? Very. Regardless, it's a level of confidence I wish could be bottled for a rainy day, because it is inevitable—the clouds *will* roll back in and my mania will be washed away in a moment, making me a shadow of the person I was just minutes before.

The highs of my mania often manifested themselves at the most unexpected times and in the most exotic places.

A Sunburn and Some Rice

It was our family's final night in Paradise. A week's worth of baking in the Mexican sun had given us all exactly what we needed—quality time together, warm temperatures, and neon pink skin to show for it. As we wrapped up our last all-you-can-maul meal, I decided to make one more pass through the buffet line with my husband in tow. Then it happened... I reached the rice and it hit me—a rushing surge of the best feelings imaginable. Uncontrollable laughter soon followed. Everything was hilarious—the rice, the Caesar salad beside it, bikini-clad vacationers sitting nearby, the palm trees outside, the entire country of Mexico. And so there I was—hysterical, unable to move or even heap a spoonful of basmati onto my plate. My husband grabbed the serving spoon and rescued my wobbling plate from falling to the floor. Things got funnier and my giggling got louder. I *loved* it—like a rush, a hit, from the most powerful drug. It was the best kind of laughter on the planet; the kind that gets you kicked out of class and sent straight to the principal's office; the kind that makes your stomach muscles ache for days. But no one was laughing along with me. It wasn't funny. *I* wasn't funny. What made my Mexican "fit" even more unsettling was that it hadn't been spurred on by a joke or embarrassing moment. It had come out of nowhere, and was only being shared between me and a giant dish of white rice.

Minutes passed before I finally got control of myself and made my way back to our table with my hubby's help. He knew the drill—I had hit a high and would soon plummet to an equal low. Embarrassed, I sat in silence as a dull headache set in. The party was over.

I never forgot that euphoric "rice high," and it is a very good thing. Years later, when recounted to a psychiatrist, it would serve as both a clue and compelling evidence and ultimately lead to a proper diagnosis.

You are a ***hurricane*** of a girl;
remember to breathe
every once in a while,
do not drown
within your own storm.

-Emma Bleker

Midnight Run
a fugitive in flip-flops

It was the middle of the night and the dead of winter, stone-cold and pitch-black, but I was in a much darker place. As I stepped outside in my flannel pajamas (penguin print, of course) and well-worn flip-flops, my mind was spinning, clouding any ounce of sound judgment I had. I unlocked my car door, jumped in, and turned the key. With one foot firmly on the brake, I used the other rubber sole of my sandal to frantically pump the gas pedal. And there I sat, feverishly revving my car engine in the driveway. My behaviour eerily echoed what I was feeling inside—surges of rage, anger, adrenaline—waves that kept crashing over me with increasing intensity.

My four-wheeled weapon of choice was parked just beneath the bedroom window where my husband lay fast asleep, blissfully unaware of the unfolding drama. Knowing he was a deep dreamer, I hoped that the roar of the engine would rouse him enough to roll over and notice he was alone; that the sheets on my side of the bed had been peeled back and my snoozing spot was empty. I wanted him to hear the screeching of tires peeling out of the driveway and the car engine fade as I drove off into the night. I was gone, in every sense of the word, and I wanted him to notice it in the most dramatic way. I was on the run—going somewhere, anywhere, nowhere. It was an incoherent cry for help that was manifesting itself as a made-for-the-movies midnight getaway.

We had fought ferociously at bedtime. I suppose I should rephrase. *I* fought. To anyone watching ringside, it was most definitely a one-sided match; my husband *never* "hit" back. A wise and tempered man, he was smart enough to know that engaging in battle with a wild animal would be foolish and only lead to more destruction. Having failed to lure my "opponent" into my dysfunctional ways, I abandoned my attempt and fell asleep on my anger. That is, until I woke a few hours later and picked up right where I had left off.

It didn't take long for my plan to fall flat. I hadn't thought it out any further than the end of our driveway—hadn't packed a blanket, toothbrush, toilet paper, tabloid magazine, or even a stick of gum. After only one block, I veered down a side street, found the parking lot of a lawn bowling club, threw the car into Park, and panicked. I knew that the instant I turned off the engine, my seat heater (which had barely begun to warm my buns) would cool and the radio fade, leaving me in freezing temperatures and silence. But it was my only option. After all, idling for as long as my fuel tank would allow would have been ridiculously suspicious.

The fear of the police driving by overshadowed everything. What would I tell them? They would surely never believe that I was only interested in some rebellious moonlight lawn bowling. Did I dare use the excuse of a docile domestic squabble or searching for a missing cat? I was terrified that the truth would send me straight to the hospital for an assessment. I fully reclined my seat and curled up, trying to find a comfortable position to conserve body heat. I held out as long as I could. After a full ten minutes, I tucked my tail between my legs, fired up the engine, and returned home. My one-woman standoff was over.

Hoping to find my husband worried sick and wildly pacing, I slowly opened the back door and walked inside. The house was dark and quiet. As I approached our bedroom I finally heard him. But instead of offering a physical description of me to the authorities to be plastered on the side of a milk carton, he was snoring. He hadn't rolled over into my empty spot, let alone even shifted his pillow or position. He had been fast asleep during the entire production and missed my Oscar-winning performance. I was so angry. All of that for nothing?

"Get. Up. Now!"

Groggy and confused, my hubby greeted me with a smile and softly said, "Hey you, is something wrong? Climb in, let's cuddle." Instead of answering, I glared and growled. Dumbfounded, my husband laid there, completely unaware of the nightmare he had just awoken into.

Once again, my "opponent" had failed to engage in battle. Admitting defeat, I waved my white flag, hopped under the covers, snuggled up beside him, and drifted off. As my husband left for work a few hours later, bewildered, he mumbled, "Hey, did you wake me in the night for something?" At that moment I decided to limit my craziness to the waking hours, when it would be seen, heard, and *remembered*.

"I hate you."

"I love you, I hate myself."

"Go away."

"Don't leave me, please stay."

"I was *fiery* and ferocious,
capable of lighting up a room
or just as easily
burning it down."

Damage and Destruction
self-sabotage

I was risking everything with my volatile words and actions, playing Russian roulette with myself and others. But why? Why such insanity, desperation, and drama? What *was* going through my mind in the moments before, during, and after my episodes?

I loved the attention and follow-up feelings my irrational indiscretions always brought. I loved having control and holding power, even if only for a few moments and for the worst reasons. There was always a rush of adrenaline. It was addictive. And I always wanted more. Just how far could I take my craziness? How risky could I be, yet still smooth things over with an apology, a romp in the sack, or some of my best behaviour? Selfish, sinister, sick, and twisted? Very. But what had set my wrecking ball in motion? Had something or someone set me off? Or, had *I* set myself off?

Often, feelings of unworthiness came from my inability to deal with the mundane—package deliveries, paying bills, school pickups, birthday parties, and even trick-or-treaters at my door. Shame and embarrassment would overwhelm me. Why were such simple things so stressful? Why couldn't I cope? It all sent me spiralling into a state of self-hate; I would become angry, frustrated, and then lash out. My outbursts would manifest themselves as middle-of-the-night getaways, verbal assaults, and, at times, even self-injury; door frames and car windows took the brunt of my frustrations, leaving me with bruised body parts.

In the seconds after my emotional explosions, my gut reaction was to run and hide—lock myself away in a bathroom, car, or closet. There was no denying who was to blame. *It was all my fault.* More than anything or anyone else, I was angry at myself, disgusted by what I had done. My thoughts ran wild and destructive self-talk raced. Every negative experience I'd ever had—being bullied, stumbling on sidewalks, failing spelling tests, brewing coffee onto kitchen counters—flooded my mind and blocked out any light at the end of the tunnel. It was a very dark place to be. I soon wanted to give up on everything and everyone—abandon all my interests and forget about friendships and family. I wanted to put an end to everything. Except, thank God, my life.

Eventually my emotions would simmer down, and my basic needs to go to the bathroom or grab a snack forced me out of hiding. I would emerge, slowly creeping out and avoiding all eye contact, trying my best to scope out the situation and assess the damage done.

My husband and children were always the innocent victims of my episodes. It was *my* train wreck, but they were caught in the wreckage with no escape.

My close friends weren't immune to my dysfunctional ways either; they often found themselves leaving unreturned phone messages, being pushed away, or locked out altogether. And sadly, I didn't have the strength to let them know that my "absence" and silence wasn't a reflection of my love, or lack thereof, for them. I was utterly incapable of looking outside myself, of seeing the forest through the trees.

Even so, against all odds, I hoped everyone would keep doing what they were doing—calling me "Mom," ringing my phone, and knocking on my door. I prayed they would be patient and wait for me to "reappear." Perhaps by then I would have the courage to tell them it was *my* problem, not theirs.

But *could* my relationships and marriage be salvaged, repaired, and restored? Eventually, the day came when I decided they couldn't.

Examine what you *tolerate*.

-Unknown

Leave Me and Never Look Back

I begged my husband to leave me; to take our children and walk away from the life we had built. I truly believed they would be better off without me, far from my destructive behaviour and dysfunctional ways. I told him that cutting me loose was his only chance of finding true happiness; of finding a woman who would love and cherish him in ways I so often couldn't. He chose to stay.

"I made a promise to you for life—I'll never leave you."

Like a broken record, my husband would regularly remind me of his pledge, hoping his words would sink deep enough into my heart and mind to convince me I was worthy of being loved, worthy of having him stay. But despite his track record—days, months, years of unconditional love and devotion—I still doubted every one of his words.

Although he never fled, or even packed his bags, it didn't mean he could stay without the help of something, or someone, outside the walls of our home.

An Online Betrayal

It was a lazy weekday morning and I was wasting time. Yes, one could easily conclude that I was being extremely effective at doing absolutely nothing. Bored out of my skull, I strolled into my husband's home office and plunked myself down in front of his computer. Operating on autopilot, I navigated toward my favourite social media sites and prepared to "like," "pin," and "post." As I waited for my intended destinations to load, my eyes caught a quick glimpse of the existing screen and its contents. It took only seconds to realize what I was seeing. I peered closer. In an instant, my heart sank, and my blood began to boil. No, it wasn't a stockpile of pornographic images or a string of racy emails to another woman. What I had found upset me even more—an active, in-session, bipolar spouse support group. Seething inside and with smoke pouring from my ears, I furiously scrolled through endless threads of desperate conversations, all describing lives of hell and heartache. And although my husband had cleverly disguised his chat name, it didn't matter; every entry was the same—a cry for help and a shoulder to lean on—and I knew he had written one of them. I. Was. Stunned. I thought I had done a stellar job of silencing him, of trapping him with no way out. After all, I had assured him that if he ever dared reach out to anyone or anything for help, *I* would walk away and never look back.

I had been betrayed. A giant steel wall instantly went up between us. How *dare* he seek the support of others, complete strangers, and do it behind my back? My online discovery also made me wonder if he had sought the help of a real-life professional, sneaking in appointments on all those days he "worked" late or during his Saturday morning "runs." I was horrified at the thought of anyone finding me out as a phony, and our family Christmas photo a fraud.

Had things really gotten that bad? Had *I* gotten that bad? I was about to find out.

What you *allow* is what will continue.

-Unknown

getting help

The Breaking Point
an ultimatum and *a lot* of pride

And that was it. I never thought my husband would ever reach a limit. I had just selfishly and arrogantly assumed he would be my punching bag for the rest of my life. I assumed wrong. He had endured fourteen years on my rollercoaster and needed to get off, or at least try to slow it down. He handed down an ultimatum that scared me to death: "Go and get help," he begged, "or I'll go, and take the kids with me and get us help." I knew he was serious. Dead serious. It was all more than he could handle; *I* was more than he could handle.

I despised the idea of finding a doctor and seeking answers; cringed at the thought of letting someone from the outside world into mine, allowing a stranger to see my weakness. I feared the worst—a diagnosis, prescribed pills, or, God forbid, being strapped to a stretcher and rolled away. Even more devastating, what if my children were the ones taken? How would I ever hide that? I couldn't. The mere thought of it all made me want to vomit. Filled with selfish pride, I wanted to keep my illness—a ticking time bomb—hidden within the walls of my home. If it exploded into the open, my dark secret would be exposed for all to see, to gossip about and gasp at. I was convinced that everyone would rally around my husband—bring him casseroles and offer condolences. And all the while I'd be left in the dust, sleeping in a padded room and sitting through therapy sessions with strip-searched roommates.

A doctor's appointment was made, and I decided it would be a fantastic idea to keep it; there would be no games of Hide and Seek this time around. I was a grown adult and needed to finally take responsibility for my actions—if not for myself, then for the sake of my family. Silently kicking and screaming, I walked into the doctor's office with my husband by my side. I was so embarrassed. To be a grown woman—a wife and a mother—and then have to tell another adult that on some days I could barely brush my teeth and pull my pants up was humiliating. I felt "less-than"—like a broken being, incapable of controlling my own thoughts and actions.

I had only been assaulted with a few prying questions before my honest answers generated an instant referral on a dreaded little piece of white paper. I'd been *sentenced* to see a psychiatrist.

I was hitting the big leagues. I insisted on driving myself and going alone. Dressed to the nines, even wearing a pair of mile-high heels, I did my best to walk confidently into the building. I was hoping to convince others I was a doctor, receptionist, or even a maintenance worker—I just needed to be *anyone* but someone who needed an assessment, straightjacket, or sedation. Once again, as they so often did, my thoughts spun wildly, and negative self-talk raced. Feeling judged by every person I passed, I avoided all eye contact. Things got even worse as my path through the building and elevator floor number gave glaring clues as to where I was headed and why.

A Psychiatrist and a Search Party
"liar, liar, pants on fire"

I'm a liar. Yes, it's true. I lied, straight to the face of a psychiatrist, in response to one of the most serious questions I might ever be asked in my life:

"Have you ever, in your darkest moments, had thoughts of taking your own life?"

"No, never," I immediately answered, without flinching a facial muscle. (I'm sure if that doctor gets his hands on this book and reads this admission of dishonesty, he'll send out a search party by sundown.)

The truth is, so many of my days were spent worrying about anything and everything, hour by hour, minute to minute. I would lay my head on my pillow each night mentally and emotionally exhausted. Feelings of sadness, frustration, and anger would envelop me and make life seem as if it would always be an uphill battle. I longed for stillness, for even one minute without worrying. Yes, it was in those moments that I *did* have a fleeting thought of how I could find permanent peace.

But that's as far as I ever let my mind go. I never (*never, ever, ever*) went so far as to imagine how or when; positive thoughts always won over any urges to "end it." Darkness was instantly illuminated and overpowered by memories of the past and dreams for the future—of falling in love, taking out a mortgage, making babies, and of one day watching my children walk down the aisle and say "I do" to their own fairy tale futures. I would remind myself of fancy dinners shared with friends, long walks on warm summer nights, and all those tropical vacations when I was buried alive on the beach and left with grains of sand lingering in unreachable nooks and crannies for twenty-four hours (and just as many showers) later. I had, and have, so much to live for. "Never do in the darkness what can't be undone when the light returns." Such wise words I once heard and have never forgotten. The light *always, eventually* returns. And now, back to sitting in the pyschiatrist's chair.

About an hour later, after being bombarded with what seemed like six thousand questions about my sex drive, sleeping habits, and self-injury, I had given the guy in the white coat all he needed to generate what my husband had been hoping and praying for—a proper diagnosis: *bipolar II disorder.*

More embarrassment, shame, humiliation. My only perceptions of bipolar disorder were negative; online searches always turned up disturbing images of tormented souls and cartoons with twisted smiles, but never pictures of people who seemed to be living "normal," productive, happy lives. I only thought of my diagnosis as a death sentence of sorts, a warning label that carried "contents under pressure" and "easily flammable" warnings so others could keep a safe distance. I was convinced my disorder was a burden and a secret I would have to carry and keep for the rest of my life.

But regardless of my initial reactions, my husband and I finally had an earth-shattering explanation for my troubled existence and the hope that life could be better. But would I be willing to take the advice given and pills prescribed?

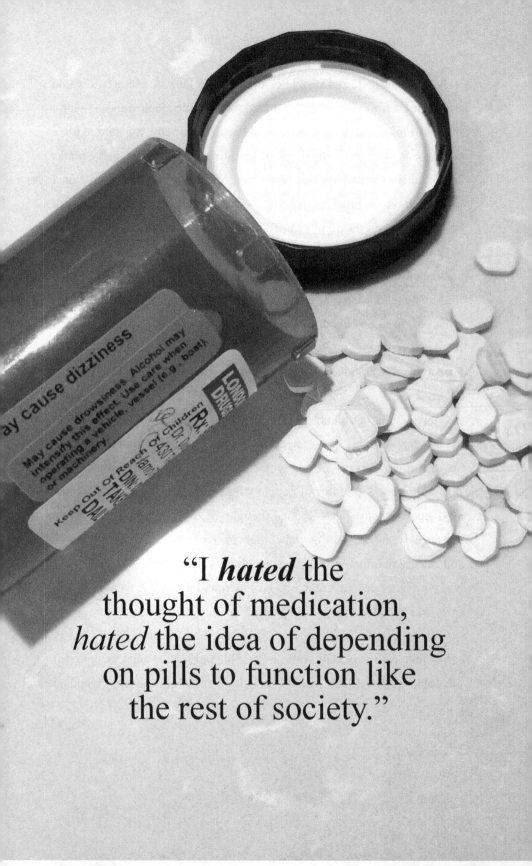

"I *hated* the thought of medication, *hated* the idea of depending on pills to function like the rest of society."

Pill Popping
prescribed pills and a course of action

Hate is a very strong word. I've taught my children *never* to use it. I HATED the thought of medication, *hated* the idea of depending on pills to function like the rest of society. Would medicine merely mask symptoms or sedate my emotions? Would it offer a cure or just a cover-up? Besides, although for different reasons— the prevention of parenthood and anxious thoughts—I had gone the prescription drug route in the past, with pathetic results and far too many side effects.

There were parts of my bipolarity that I loved and didn't want to lose—my creative manic episodes of writing and painting for weeks on end without a wink of sleep or ounce of self-doubt. I wasn't interested in living a boring existence, with flat-lining emotions or foam flowing from my mouth. What if I became a zombie with no zest for life? Once again, the thought of it all made me want to throw up.

But this time, my situation was different and dire. I was a mess and on the brink of losing everything—my family, friendships, sanity, even my life. I had been treading water far too long and was exhausted, drowning, and incapable of saving myself. I needed a lifeline thrown from a professional whose medical know-how was far more trustworthy than my own. It was going to take much more than a new pair of shoes or some positive thinking for me to keep my head above water, catch my breath, and make it safely to shore.

My psychiatrist and family doctor both gave me their educated advice, and I took it, along with the mood-stabilizing medication they prescribed. Yes, I've chosen the "happy-pill path." Now, I need to be brutally honest here—the pills haven't made me, or life, perfect. My moods are not always stable. I can still fly off the handle (not to be confused with handle bars, biking accident, remember?), and I do have down days. But life is *so much better* than ever before. Side effects are minimal, my moods are more manageable, and so, for the foreseeable future, I'm staying the course.

heading in a new direction

Twenty Questions and a Seed Sown

It was a fun way to pass the time. Instead of idle girl-talk about removing unsightly body hair or smoothing our socially acceptable ones, a friend suggested we play a game of Twenty Questions... far less risky than Truth or Dare and much more age-appropriate. I was *all in*, an enthusiastic participant, willing to answer whatever was asked.

"If you were given unlimited time and resources to make this world a better place, what would you do?"

I pondered my reply, wanting my answer to be a meaningful one. I had always struggled to find my true purpose in life; I wanted my time on earth to count for more, to reach far beyond the small radius around me. Deep down, I knew there was a more significant way to spend my waking hours than just lurking around on social media sites—I just needed to find it. I had so much more to offer the world than just a few clever status updates or a free "pay-it-forward" meal to that lone guy behind me in the drive-thru (who, as it turned out, was ordering food for an *entire* sports team). But despite years of endlessly searching for my purpose, I never found it. There were fumbles and false starts, failures and perceived defeats, all ending in utter frustration. My aimless grasping often threw me off balance and into deep holes of depression. But I would always eventually claw myself out—sometimes on my own and other times with the help of loved ones or prescribed pills. Unfortunately, my shame and humiliation over my inability to handle the basics—driving, getting fuel, ordering fast food—often overshadowed any progress I made. No sooner had I made it back to safe ground than I would find myself falling back into a pit of self-pity.

I tethered almost every ounce of self-worth to things outside myself—a high-powered career, a part-time job, even a flimsy, self-printed business card. None of which I had.

Breaking out in hives was an annual event for me in the hours before my husband's office Christmas parties. The mere thought of alcohol-laced conversations and prying personal questions made me roll on extra-strength deodorant beforehand. And it would always come... that dreaded question: "So, what do you do?"

"Uh, duh, nothing... I'm just a mom," I would always nervously mumble. With no resumé to send over, I even underestimated my ability to carry on a conversation, fearful of seeming uneducated and less eloquent than my fellow partygoers, even in their drunken states. To add insult to injury, I was sure to follow up my "just a mom" response with a few run-on sentences of self-deprecation. I did it *every* time, *every* year, and then beat myself up for weeks afterward. And now, back to that rousing round of Twenty Questions.

It had only been a few months since my diagnosis, but my game partner was a close friend who knew me well; I took comfort in knowing that my answer wouldn't carry much shock, if any:

"I'd like to get to a place where I could share about my disorder, to hopefully help others and be some small part of taking away the fear and misunderstanding of mental illness."

With every ounce of my being, I hoped the stigma and stereotypes would one day disappear or at least fade. And deep down, I knew if I was willing to lay aside my pride and be vulnerable, I could somehow be a small part of that happening. But I was nowhere near ready. I was having enough trouble just remembering to take my medication every night... so far from a place of being able to "out" myself to the world, let alone my own friends and family.

Our game ended soon after, but my answer wasn't forgotten. A seed, although small and in need of time to take root and grow, had been sown in my heart and mind with one off-the-cuff question.

a 5,000-mile move across the world later...

Insurance Coverage Denied
"do I qualify for coverage, or just as being *crazy*?"

I was just wrapping up an in-person meeting with a German insurance agent, just one of the many tasks of setting up my new European existence.

"Any psychological conditions?" he stoically asked.

"Nope!" I nervously chirped, as he reached the end of his questionnaire. Yuck. No sooner had he left my apartment than my conscience kicked in and prompted me to stare (I certainly wouldn't have called it reading) at the application's fine print. Despite my German language skills being zilch, there were a few words—*manisch depressiv* and *psyche*—that looked eerily familiar. I felt sick inside. Once again, I had proven myself to be dishonest by lying straight to someone's face. Riddled with guilt and knowing I needed to come clean, I penned a pathetic letter in a feeble attempt to fess up (opposite page in italics, be sure to read it right now).

Far too many words, an excessive amount of exclamation marks, an inappropriate smiley face, and even *more* lies. After all, no dose of bipolar medication, no matter how low, would have ever been passed over a pharmacist's counter into my hands without me having an official diagnosis, prescription slip, and a doctor's signature. My deception didn't end there. *Manic depression* is a name that is absolutely interchangeable with *bipolar,* and The Diagnostic and Statistical Manual of Mental Disorders (DSM) is a handbook used by health care professionals around

Hi Dieter!

*Just had a chance to glance over the German life insurance application, and although 99% of it has left me at a loss to understand, I suppose I know enough German at this point to recognize the word "psyche!" Thought it definitely worth letting you know that I am currently on a low dose of medication used to treat bipolar II disorder. I noticed that the term **manic-depressive** is used on the application. I believe this term might be interchangeable with, and has now been replaced by **bipolar** in the DSM used by psychiatrists in Canada. I am not sure if this diagnostic manual is the same worldwide. Needless to say, I am sure that this may affect my application and rates, assuming I qualify for coverage at all!!*

Thanks so much!!!
Julie :)

the world... and I knew it. Who was I trying to fool? If it was Dieter, it didn't work. *Nothing* had been lost in translation.

Within minutes of sending my message, my phone began to ring. Although I *was* fully expecting a response to my bombshell admission, did it have to be so soon? And by phone? I had hoped his reply would be electronic, so I could digest it privately and keep some of my dignity intact if need be. My heart sank. I knew he wasn't calling to invite me to his birthday party or out for schnitzel. Was it really that serious? Was having bipolar disorder that big of a deal breaker? I was about to find out.

With all my defenses up, I begrudgingly answered his call in my most convincing "yes-I-have-my-life-together" voice. Dieter, a stranger to me just twenty-four hours before, now knew one of my deepest, darkest secrets. Filtered through my insecurity and embarrassment, his voice seemed condescending, s-l-o-w-e-r than ever before, as he broke the news that I was no longer eligible for insurance and then tried to explain why. Like salt dumped on a snail or poured into a gaping wound, his words continued, "Unfortunately, folks like you are the ones who tend to drive into brick walls, at full speed." It happens rarely, but in that moment I was speechless. There was no mistaking what he had said or how hurtful it was. Nothing could have softened the blow of such an insensitive and ignorant generalization about *folks* like me. It was painful proof of how others, whether it be companies or their employees, viewed an illness that I had. As the call continued, with fists and teeth clenched, I lied to him once again. "I understand." In the same breath, I tried to defend my disorder (and myself) by explaining that the bipolar spectrum is broad, ranging from, sadly, those who take their own lives, to those who have the occasional "Manic Monday" and a few sleepless nights. I wanted to convince him that I was "normal," safe, a good person, and a great mom. And despite my unworthiness of his insurance package, I *was* worthy of everything else, including an invitation to his birthday party. Unfortunately, my efforts were in vain; Dieter didn't have the time or interest. Bottom line, he was selling a policy with rigid rules and having bipolar disorder broke them. My voice quivered as I ended the call and tears began to fall. I. Was. Humiliated.

As a society, we need to create a cultural environment in which people are encouraged to seek help when they need it—regardless of whether it is a mental illness or any other illness. *No one* should have to hide out of fear of negative consequences or reprisals such as loss of employment or social ridicule.

-Mary Giliberti
Chief Executive Officer, NAMI

Painting a New Picture

...with a pencil and some paper

Why such negative perceptions? Why is it far easier to tell a co-worker you're leaving the office early to see your dentist than your psychiatrist? Why is the media so quick to splash the craziest parts of mental illness on every cover? And why are senseless tragedies often instantly blamed on mental illness, when there are so many different factors that could be the cause? *Crazy* is a quick and easy explanation, a tempting sale, bought by many without batting an eyelash. But at what cost? A very high price, indeed.

It's time to start selling and buying *sanity*. If we don't, the story will never change; pictures, depicting *us folk* with dark circles under sad eyes, crouched in corners, clutching our heads in our hands, will continue to circulate. Others will view us and our "illnesses" that way. Far too much weight will be given to those photos, easily overshadowing, or erasing altogether, any images of us living productive lives—with genuine smiles, healthy marriages, functioning families, lifelong friendships, and impressive professional achievements. Instead, let positive photos be the ones posted, the footage played, so the world will see *us* with new eyes and a balanced perspective. And so, in the wake of that devastating insurance denial...

Dieter, and the world, needed a new picture, a different point of reference. Could I possibly be the person to give it? Deep down, I knew I could offer a glimpse (even if only a small one) into a world that is often misrepresented, misunderstood, feared, and hidden. *If* I was willing to lay aside my pride and be vulnerable, there was a chance that my authenticity could open minds, soften hearts, shatter stigma, encourage others, or (at the very least) evoke the words, "I'm not the only one." It soon became clear to me it was no longer a question of *if*, only *how* and *when*.

Easier said than done. Did I really have the guts to put it all out there? Expose myself, my husband, and my children in such a vulnerable way? After all, this wasn't just my story to tell; it was, and is, just as much their journey, their heartache, their pain. I needed to be sensitive to the wounds that writing this book could reopen, expose, or create. And most important of all, I needed to wait for their blessing. They soon gave it. And then, there was nothing standing in my way but myself.

Ernest Hemingway once said, "There is nothing to writing, all you do is sit down at a typewriter and bleed." Eventually, the day came when my firm belief that my journey was one worth sharing overshadowed and outweighed my fear of not being capable of doing so. It was time to take a deep breath, cast my insecurities aside, and "bleed," as openly and honestly as I could. And so, with the unconditional love and support of my family and a few close friends, I sat down and began to write.

"In the realm of mental illness there are myriad examples of *recovery*, lives rebuilt and inspirational examples of people making a real difference to the society they are living in. Our media needs to reflect this reality more clearly and to help shift perception to where it should be–informed by facts and not by fear."*

*BLOG: An Uneasy Awakening: Bipolar Musings
www.uneasyawakening.com/2014/10/26/mental-illness-the-media-time-for-reflection/

a few months and 5,000 lattes later...

Out of the Closet and Off a Cliff

As a much-needed distraction from writing, and an incredible sign of optimism, I took a creative detour. I put my manuscript on the back burner and began to "brew" a book trailer of sorts. And so began the process of fumbling around with a fancy camera and talking to a teddy bear. As ridiculous as it sounds, it's true. While my kids were away at school, I tried to mimic the making of a million dollar documentary and create Hollywood magic, all from the comfort of my very own home. With my camera precariously perched on an ironing board and slanted stack of books, I recorded days of footage. Yes, doing my best to keep a straight face, I locked eyes and shared my story with a stuffed animal instead of a human being.

Unfortunately, one "take" was never enough. Neither were five or fifty. Murphy's law and logic proved that no sooner had I finished filming an impressive run of footage—sentences perfectly formed and enunciated—than I would discover that the Record button hadn't been pressed properly. Just as frustrating, despite focusing the camera beforehand, my head bobbing and arm flailing often created footage so blurry it would have sent viewers straight to the optometrist for extensive eye exams. Now, if I *did* manage to keep the frame in focus, the undeniable wail of a European siren would inevitably creep into the shot, creating a sound effect that was impossible to eliminate.

And this makes no mention of the hours of editing that were lost in an instant, courtesy of a software fritz and a few "forced quits." But I didn't give up. I fought through and finished. And then, in a split second of bravery (and after notifying my next of kin), I posted my full-disclosure documentary, *The Other Side of Me,** for the *entire* world to see.

It seemed as if everyone—my husband's co-workers, potential employers, parents of my friends and friends of my parents, not to mention my inlaws and the neighbour's cousin's mother's brother's cat—had seen my video, or at least heard about it. (Un)reliable sources say I was the "talk of the town." But what could people say that I hadn't already said myself? Publicly declaring I was a train wreck and offering supporting evidence left no hidden secrets to fuel the rumour mill. Even so, I felt vulnerable, and worried what reactions would come my way.

Feeling as if I had leaped off the tallest cliff without a parachute, I braced for the worst. I didn't need too. My inbox was instantly flooded with messages of love and support from close friends, as well as complete strangers. The compassion of others "caught" me, and to this day brings me to tears and to my knees. It is inspiring proof that acceptance and empathy abound.

But were my intentions pure? Did I secretly love all the attention? And for all the wrong reasons?

Seek to be *worth knowing* rather than be well known.

-Sandra Turley

* www.youtube.com/channel/UCFio8QFp1L3cfq8gFZqnSQQ

Checking My Motives

Am I a "fame whore?" (I honestly wasn't sure if I would be able to work that word into my memoir.) It's a loaded and legitimate question that I've been asked more than once. It is also one I've asked myself while pondering my motives for writing this tell-all. *Am I* in the midst of a midlife crisis? *Is* this a desperate attempt to seek attention, fame, and fortune, at any cost, even if it's by making a public spectacle of myself? My answer to all these inquiries is a simple and confident, "I don't think so."

Now, it *is* true that throughout my school years I was an enthusiastic member of drama clubs and theatre productions. And, on my "good" days, I've never been one to shy away from a camera, an empty stage, or a microphone. But, with the exception of singing onstage with a musical superstar (that was purely to fulfill a lifelong dream and my own selfish desires), the purposes of my performances have always been to encourage, inspire, and bring attention to things other than myself. So, instead of characterizing it as seeking the spotlight, it's more a case of not turning away if it shines in my direction and can be used in meaningful ways. If *my* "mug" can somehow help to change the face of what is still such a feared and misunderstood "illness" or add a bit of balance to a scale so heavily weighted with stigma, then dim the lights and start the cameras rolling. Go right ahead, slap my story on the front page of the newspaper *and* the six o'clock news.

A Sensitive Soul and Some Rejection

Rejection. I should have been expecting it. After all, posting a video that showcased me and mental illness, instead of double rainbows or cats doing cartwheels, was a huge risk. So, of course, it happened. Someone saw my video, decided "no thanks," and hit "dislike." The mere thought of another human being walking the face of the earth and not thinking of me fondly was devastating. You can imagine how distressing the next two "thumbs down" were, followed by a malicious comment.

I. Was. Crushed.

I spent days afterward desperately trying to make sense of the rejection. Was it because of my collared shirt or shade of hair? Tone of voice or choice of vocabulary? The background music? Did I remind someone of their nosy neighbour, an ex-girlfriend, or monster mother-in-law? Over the next few days, I fearfully checked my posted video for the number of views and amount of disapproval it had received. I debated irrational actions of self-preservation—deleting it, abandoning my writing efforts, going into a cave and never coming out. I was convinced that, as a human, I was highly offensive and extremely hateable.

I wasn't only leery of virtual rejection, I was also terrified of what real-life people were thinking of me, during the week and even on a Sunday morning.

Take Me to Church
a fraudulent faith?

It would be hypocritical to not mention what is most important to me—my faith in God. It shapes the lens through which I view the world, motivating my actions or lack thereof.

As a pastor's kid, I spent every Sunday morning wearing a smocked dress and sitting in a church pew. My decision to become a Christian was made at a very young age, and although questioned at times, it's one that has stuck. Since then, I've tried to live my life accordingly, striving to keep God first in all things and practice what I preach.

But was I brainwashed as a child, and now just blindly following in the footsteps of my father? Be assured, I've explored other religions, asked many questions, and sought my own answers. I have decided for myself what I believe and why, and whether I'm going to crawl out of bed on a Sunday morning or roll over and go back to sleep.

Why do I believe? To put it simply, there is too much around me to suggest there *is* a God—the sight of newborn babies (especially my own), majestic mountain ranges, breathtaking sunsets, the intricate patterns on butterflies' wings, inner workings of the human brain, and the list goes on (and on, and on). It all leaves me awestruck and in wonder.

So yes, it would be *more than safe* to assume that I absolutely do believe in God. I also believe that the Bible is His true spoken word, filled with teachings that transcend time and are as powerful today as they were thousands of years ago. Yes, there are gaps—questions that science and logic can't explain—and I choose to fill them in with my faith. So, instead of magic pennies or strokes of luck, I believe in miracles and angels among us. In my mind, we are *more* than mere beings whose lives and deaths have no eternal matter or meaning. *So much more.*

But despite my youthful pledge to stick to the "straight and narrow," I'm *far* from perfect. I have stumbled and fallen... said and done things that were inconsistent with my faith that have left me guilt-ridden and full of regret, doubting my worthiness of forgiveness and grace. I've had moments of feeling close to God, but others of feeling so very far away. At times, I've questioned His ways, His promises, and even His very existence. After all, why would God create me with a mental illness; burden me with such deep struggles? How could that possibly be any part of His divine plan for my life? Doubts would creep in. Was my disorder real or my faith fake? *Was* it possible for a church-going chick to also be battling debilitating depression and anxiety? Why didn't I feel the same peace and joy as my fellow believers? Why wasn't God's assurance that I could cast my cares on Him enough to "cure" me? Was my faith all I should have needed to fight my fears? Thank goodness, I've since put (most of) my doubts, fears, and questions to rest. Through it all, although tested and shaken, my faith has remained.

I have now come to realize that God doesn't promise, or owe, us an existence of ease, one without struggles and hardship. Life *isn't* fair. Sadly, bad things do happen to good people. God does promise, however, that if He can't calm life's storms, then He will calm and carry *us* through them.

When you go through
deep waters,
I will be with you.
When you go through
rivers of difficulty,
you will not drown...

Isaiah 43:2a NLT

He will cover you
with his feathers.
He will *shelter* you
with his wings.
His faithful promises
are your armor
and protection.

Psalm 91:4 NLT

The truth is, I haven't always been open to God's helping hand. Stubborn and proud, I've often relied on my own strength to get by. My bad—*my* problem, not His. God never leaves us out in the cold. He has given us resources and tools—doctors, counselors, medicine, and more—to help us navigate our struggles. All we need to do is use wisdom and discernment over how and when we use them.

But although I have come to a place of peace with my faith, it doesn't mean I've always been comfortable spending my Sunday mornings in a chapel.

Unfortunately, in some minds, the Church and its members have become known for harsh judgment and hypocrisy; thought of as an organization of people who profess to believe one thing, yet often do another. Yes, I'm talking about a handful of those little old church ladies with crocheted purses, who cast cruel condemnation on all those who cross their paths. I must admit, I was most fearful of my "own."

How *did* my fellow Christians view me? As a wounded, broken bird in desperate need of healing? And my mental illness? Was it seen as a sign of unconfessed sin or a spiritual battle raging within my soul? In the wake of my video "confession," I am thrilled to report that my fears of being cast out of the congregation were quickly put to rest; my fellow Christians were kind and compassionate, and embraced me with open arms and minds.

Pastors *are* talking about mental illness from the pulpit, and many have opened up about their own personal struggles. Discussions are being started, conversations had, and most important of all, people are feeling the freedom to seek solace within the Church. After all, the Church is also known for helping people in their hour of greatest need. Mental illness should be and, thankfully, is now becoming no exception.

We judge because we *don't* understand.

-Unknown

instructions and advice

Suspicious Behaviour and Tough Love
get help and have hope

Maybe you now suspect that you too have bipolar disorder, or something similar. Perhaps you only needed to read some of my tell-tale signs and symptoms to recognize your own.

At first or fiftieth glance, this illness can easily be overlooked or passed off as passion, explosive creativity, a rough patch, a burst of energy, insomnia, anxiety, or an anger management issue (not to mention a bad hair day, PMS, or the fault of a full moon). If you're feeling a little "off," if things seem "outta-wack," don't deny it. I'm guessing most of us wouldn't brush aside a broken bone or sudden loss of sight, and then just cross our fingers and hope for healing. Our mental health needs to be given the same care and attention as our physical well-being; instead of shrugging things off, take steps toward making repairs. And no, this does not mean completing a six-question, six-second questionnaire or speed-reading an unreliable blog. A self-diagnosis will *not* suffice.

There is hope and help, in all shapes and sizes: doctors, counselors, friends, faith, books, *reliable* blogs, exercise, medication, meditation, and yes, even in the simple knowledge that *you are not alone*. That's right, I'm right alongside, and will be for the rest of my days.

Needing help *isn't* a sign of weakness, and seeking help *is* a sign of incredible strength. Reach out. Let someone in, whether it's with a shout or a whisper. And, if you don't have the strength or desire to do it for yourself (I sure didn't), do it for the sake and sanity of those around you. It won't be easy—anything in life worth having, worth fighting for, rarely is—but it will be worth it. It could be the difference between salvaging your marriage, keeping friendships, holding down a job, upholding your reputation, saving your life, or *losing it all*.

Dig Deeper

When I was first given my diagnosis, I was completely overwhelmed. I had no desire to drown myself in definitions, study statistics, or research remedies.

Inform yourself. Do as I say, *not* as I did. Hypocritical? Very. There was, and is, no excuse for me not to research my disorder and learn more. No longer afraid of what I might discover, with diligence and discernment, I'm now reading books (hard to believe, I know), "following" blogs, watching documentaries, and connecting with people walking similar paths. It's my very best chance of gaining insight and understanding, of seeing the full picture, and ultimately helping my doctors find the most effective treatment for me.

Don't let a diagnosis be the end of your journey; it gives your pain a name and a reason, but it's just a starting point. You've only just begun.

Open Your Heart to Me

That fateful game of Twenty Questions continued with question number nine:

"What quality do you value most in a person?"

Before thinking too long, I answered, "Authenticity." In hindsight, there are a few other traits perched higher on my list, but those are assumed chart-toppers.

Despite all our best efforts to appear as if we have it all together and wake up with fresh breath, I don't think many of us actually do (I surely don't). Even so, it seems that authenticity is nearly impossible to find—people who are willing to strip down and, yes, run in rush hour naked. It is so refreshing to meet someone who is brave enough to be "real" and admit when they are scared, insecure, nervous, or embarrassed. Stumbling across authenticity is a gift, an opportunity to fast-forward past "Christmas party small-talk" and get to the heart of who someone *really* is.

Take a risk. Roll the dice. Yes, vulnerability can open us up to hurt and heartache, but it can also open the door to lasting relationships when we find folks willing to do the same. Being transparent with others is our very best chance of having it reciprocated. When people who are willing to be vulnerable cross paths, the most beautiful bonds can be formed; ones that are firmly rooted and rarely found in a world full of hardened hearts and masked faces.

Unmasked

My mask is off. And thankfully, the pressure's off too—to parallel park, cook, and slather on six layers of make-up every morning to hide my less-than-perfect skin. There is no need to impress anyone, and I can show up for a coffee date as *just Julie,* whether I'm happy, sad, or "running off the rails."

I'm not playing the blame game anymore, either. *I own it all.* Ultimately we are all responsible for ourselves and our actions. It is so tempting to use our deficits, hardships, or disorders as a go-to crutch; an excuse for poor decisions and bad behaviour; as justification for our misery and a reason to wallow in self-pity. That is, by far, the easier road to take, and I'm trying my best not to travel it.

Even better? I can't live in denial. Writing my story has forced me to delve into every area of my life—past and present—to revisit my proudest moments, but also my biggest mistakes. Not only am I more self-aware, everyone else has now been fully briefed on my journey also. It's a good thing. A *very* good thing. My hiding spots are fewer and further between, and I can't get away with any of my old tricks. Thank goodness, my gig is finally up.

But best of all, I'm not out on my own. I've got a new fan club of folks who now know of my struggles and are cheering me on, willing to offer listening ears, speak encouraging words, cook casseroles for my family, and even give me a few hand slaps if need be. They all make me accountable. I want to *do* better and *be* better. Once again, it's a *very* good thing.

Having bipolar disorder might be a reason, but it should never be an *excuse*.

-Unknown

Be *gentle* with yourself,
you're doing the best you can.

-Unknown

Cut Yourself Some Slack

For so long I was convinced I was on my own, the only one struggling. I had been completely fooled into believing that my hairdresser, barista, and the neighbourhood dog walker all had their ducks (and dogs) in a row. No one else in the entire universe seemed to be hiding behind a mask, bolted front door, or disconnected phone, *but me.*

"Nobody's perfect." I've heard the expression, the supposedly comforting one-liner, for years. And now, I finally believe it. Whether it's Sally up the street or Bob around the bend, everyone has *something*—high cholesterol, irritable bowel syndrome, a monobrow, mental illness, and more. Sometimes our struggles are exposed for all to see and other times they are hidden behind closed doors (or drastically altered with a pair of tweezers). We all have deficits—things we would never mention during a job interview or on a first date.

Don't beat yourself up (or down) for your slip-ups—for the odd outburst or some middle-of-the-night mayhem. A few minutes of madness don't define or doom any of us. We are not the sum of our worst moments. And, although we might not be eligible for life insurance, we will always qualify for unconditional love, acceptance, forgiveness, and grace—whether it's from God, family, friends, ourselves, or even the neighbour's cousin's mother's brother's cat. Please (I'm begging), allow me to remind you, and myself, that my infamous midnight run and Mexican giggle fit total just two days of my entire existence. Even better, those actual episodes account for only about one hour out of my forty-two years. The rest of my 15,000 days have been filled with amazing moments that have created lasting memories, the really great kind. I've had the privilege and honour of sitting in board rooms, serving on committees, speaking on stages, and teaching in classrooms. Even more important, I have three beautiful children, who still acknowledge me in the schoolyard, still raid my closet on a regular basis, and, most importantly, still call me "Mom." And I honestly do believe that my husband might even say my kissing skills would steam up any big screen.

Keeping Good Company
an impressive list

Thank goodness, bipolar disorder does not discriminate. It doesn't prevent people from being highly successful in their personal and professional lives. People living with bipolar disorder are caring, loving, passionate, creative, and imaginative, and the list goes on (and on, and on). We are mothers and fathers, doctors, lawyers, art directors, humanitarians, baristas, presidents, dog walkers, scientists, CEOs, concert pianists, caregivers, journalists, and more. Once again, the impressive list is endless.

Of course, the curious cat in me decided to find out if anyone well-known was walking the same path. Much to my delight, an impressive group of people popped up—famous artists, world-renowned writers, legendary leaders, award-winning actors, soulful singers, and even an astronaut—all people who have made incredible contributions to science, society, and even outer space. I'm keeping very good company.

Take it Slow

seeing how the pieces fit

The questions I ask myself on a daily basis are neverending and range from silly to serious. Did I remember to take the price tag and size sticker off my pants? Would my morning breath seduce someone or strip wallpaper? (It's actually not that bad.) *Am* I making a difference with my life? Will my existence ultimately change the world for the better, or worse?

At the risk of sounding incredibly cheesy, I wholeheartedly believe that each of us has been placed on this planet for a purpose—it may be as big as becoming president or as seemingly small as starting a game of Twenty Questions. Regardless, never underestimate your significance or impact on others and the world. Everyone has a story that can make a difference, *if* they are willing to take a leap of faith and tell it. Be brave. Dare to ask how you can use your life—all of it—the good and bad, joys and heartaches, failures and successes. The possibilities are limitless. Do it any way and anywhere—on paper, online, or in person; and whether you're in a full body cast or standing in the centre of the cereal aisle. Sorry, I'm not easing up. *You're* on the hook because no one can share your experiences more authentically than you.

If it's mental health you're able to shed light on, you can offer a new perspective and the inside scoop. Even more exciting, if you're able to give a glimpse of what getting help looks like, you can become living proof for others that life *can* be better. The more stories of hope and healing that emerge, the higher the odds that others will stumble across them, learn from them, and have the courage to seek help.

Just slow down, don't get *your* granny panties tied in a knot. There is no need to rush your story or its timing. You don't have to spill your guts today or tomorrow; only *when* you're ready, and only *if* you're ready. Just look at me. I am, without a doubt, the epitome of a late bloomer. After all, it did take me almost four decades to find my purpose. "Better late than never" is the expression, right? I finally figured it out and discovered how my overactive and imaginative mind could best be put to use. I decided to start writing. The problem was, and I considered it to be a major one, despite penning school essays and an embarrassing number of unrequited love letters, I'd never considered myself a writer. No, I never had the desire to write a book or become a published author. What I did have, however, was my story, and the passionate belief I should tell it.

As I began to write this book, it was such a relief to realize I hadn't missed any signs or signals of what I should be spending my days doing. I hadn't been oblivious to the obvious, and there was no lost time to make up for. My daily mishaps and adventures, successes and failures, and ups and downs had all been preparing me, changing me, breaking me, bringing me to my knees, and then building me back up to a place of being strong enough to share.

I can't take much of the credit, either. It wasn't all my doing. As I look back now, I realize that so many amazing people and events have all played a part in this book becoming a reality. A game of questions played at just the right time, with someone who asked just the right ones. A few unintentionally humorous emails of mine that were met with rave reviews and followed up with the enthusiastic advice, "You should write!" "Get out into the world and show people how gifted and talented you are," ordered another friend. So many seeds had unknowingly been planted and watered by others' unsolicited and unbiased votes of confidence in me.

My journey has been one giant jig-saw puzzle. It took God (not magic or coincidence) to bring all the pieces and people into my life, years for me to fit them together, and perspective to see the picture they were creating. And then, of course, all I needed was a pen, some paper, a caffeine drip, and the courage to expose myself to the *entire* world.

You are not here just to fill space or be the background character in someone else's movie. Nothing would be the same if you did not exist. Every place you have ever been and every person you have ever spoken to would be different without *you*. We are all connected and we are all affected by the decisions and existence of those around us.

-David Niven

gentle reminders

Getting and Giving Respect

the joke is *not* on me

I live in a house full of pranksters and can handle a joke *most* of the time. I've always been an easy (and willing) target, and until recently, my disorder was not immune. There was relentless teasing about "happy" pills, padded walls, straight jackets, and tiger blood. And Christmastime was always good for a few wisecracks about riding the Bi-Polar Express. I would try my best to be a great sport, but must admit, every fifth time, my feelings were hurt, deeply. I finally said, "No more." It worked. All joking about my disorder has since ceased. But not to worry, the laughter within the walls of my home won't be disappearing, or even fading, anytime soon. Be assured, there will never be a shortage of (less offensive) opportunities to make fun of me.

But my family can't take all the blame for such insensitivity about my disorder. For a split-second, I'm shifting the spotlight toward society as a whole. Too often, the word *bipolar* is loosely thrown around, used as an adjective, to describe bratty kids, hormonal teens, moody girlfriends, ornery wives, and unpredictable people. It's time to pull out a dictionary and find a different descriptor.

Others can't take all the blame, either. I'm going to stop pointing my finger in every direction *but* mine. Embarrassingly, I, too, am guilty of using less-than-flattering terms and phrases in regard to my mental health. Whether out of shame, nervousness, or sheer habit, I've often defaulted to self-deprecation, disclaimers, even *crazy* eye-rolling, all in an effort to make others feel comfortable around me. Not anymore. It is just as important for those of us living with mental illness to be acutely aware of how we speak of ourselves and our disorders. Others *will* take our lead and view our mental health the same way we do. Enough said.

*A special note for all those
living and loving alongside.

watch your mind

you're just having a bad day,
at least you're not... (insert
thousands of possibilities).

did you forget your meds?

snap out of it.

it's a choice.
just decide to be happy.

... and your mouth

did you forget to read your
Bible and say your
bedtime prayers?

first world problems,
quit whining.

you just need to take a nap.

you just need a few bottles of
wine (before breakfast).

the life I'm now living

A Small Fish in a Big Pond

A once-in-a-lifetime opportunity knocked on my family's door. We welcomed it with open arms, renewed our passports, and moved halfway around the world.

As a self-admitted Nervous Nelly, someone who defaults to what's familiar, living abroad stretched me far beyond my comfort zone. I was surrounded by new sights, sounds, and smells—all of them foreign and some downright offensive. I learned not to look twice when grannies cycled by at warp speed wearing knee-high socks with sandals on scorching summer days. And I soon discovered that the sight of dogs dining in five-star restaurants was a far more common occurrence than the regular use of razors and roll-on deodorant. Yes, I was reminded by the minute that I was a very small fish floundering around in an extremely large pond. I wouldn't have had it any other way. It was a temporary existence that I loved, and I didn't want to squander a single second or sniff.

Most notable of all, living in Europe was an adventure I would have either hated (there's that harsh word again) or passed up altogether just a few years earlier. Without having sought help and taken steps toward taming my disorder, I would have missed out on one of the most amazing experiences of my life.

Here Comes the Sun

a small pair by the pool

It had been my best tropical holiday by a million miles; I had soaked up every second of sun in the South China seas. And, although I didn't snorkel, scuba dive, or get a tan, I saw vibrant green rice fields, sipped the world's most expensive coffee, and even took an elephant for a spin. I also ventured into the depths of a monkey forest for an unexpected, aromatic anatomy lesson. It was an exposé of sorts, that fully featured the not-so-private parts of one wild ape. He started on top of my head, and things went south from there, literally. Yes, it was a most unfortunate full-frontal face swipe, that left a lingering scent even twenty-four hours (and just as many showers) later.

But there were definitely limits to my adventurous side. I still opted to flee the pool when the hunky water aerobics instructor appeared for the morning lesson. Instead of flailing in the water and working up a sweat, I watched poolside, relieved to be on dry land when the participants were ordered to link up for a Conga line. Even as medicated as I was, hopping around in a string bikini with strangers would have sent me spinning and wishing I'd given my legs an extra shave. On the bright side, as I watched from the sidelines, I no longer felt so self-conscious about my cellulite. The more ladies I saw flopping (in more ways than one) around in front

of me, the more thankful I became for my itty-bitty breasts and the fact that they are still up where they started three decades ago.

As I sat crammed in a coach seat on the flight home, most things hadn't changed. The blankets were still paper-thin, pillows germ-ridden, and headsets worth pennies. And the self-absorbed guy sitting in front of me wasted no time in fully reclining his seat, as if beckoning me to shampoo his strands in a sky-high salon. But what *had* changed was me. After only two hours in the air, I'd already used the lavatory. Twice. I had cast aside my fears of tripping or getting trapped during turbulence, and strutted down the aisle as if on a catwalk during fashion week. I was out of the closet, out of my seat, and walking 30,000 feet above the ground! The cherry on top? Hearing a string of "dings" (about 30,000) from a few seats away. Suddenly I saw an agitated flight attendant swoop in and ask a bleached blonde how on earth he could help her. Bewildered, she stared at him blankly and removed her headphones. I knew *exactly* what was happening. "Ma'am, you've been hitting the Call button like an enthusiastic contestant on a TV game show. If you're trying to adjust the volume (or win a new car), it's now a touch-screen system." I fully reclined *my* seat, grinned from ear to ear, and whispered to myself, "I'm not the only one."

ding.

"There went the sun.
The clouds can still roll
in without warning.
Here we go *again*..."

keeping it real

A Shocking Admission
November 3, 2014

Dear Diary,

Do I dare make the following shocking admission? No, I'm not having a steamy affair with the mailman or heading to pick up the keys to my new sports car. I haven't started drinking before noon or gone cold turkey off my meds. But what I am about to divulge is just as difficult to admit. I've been having a *really* hard time.

How could this be? After all, I've aired my video and am in the midst of writing my memoir to help others and offer hope. I'm *supposed* to be "better" now—calm, cool, and in control, with even my culinary skills honed to perfection. There shouldn't be anything I can't do without great ease and a big smile. And, at the very least, a friend should be able to come over for coffee without having it sampled by me first. But this hasn't been the case. Not today, yesterday, or even last week.

All I want to do is curl up in my pajamas, hot water bottle in hand, and avoid everything—friends, gas stations, cereal aisles, and the clothes in the washing machine that have been left damp for days. And my confidence in my writing abilities has vanished. I feel foolish for dreaming of being published, let alone even finishing my next sentence.

These dark and defeating feelings make no sense. None whatsoever. After all, I just spent a whirlwind week in London—sightseeing and shopping up a storm. Doing either of those things would usually invigorate me and eradicate all worries. Instead, I spent all my waking moments grouchy, anxious, and fearful of being run down by a double-decker bus or a taxi on the "wrong" side of the road. Riding the Tube was torture too. The mile-long escalators down to the trains had me crawling in my skin as I passed by thousands of commuters, all whose eyes seemed to be focused on me—staring, glaring, and questioning how I'd been granted entrance into Great Britain. Ordering a coffee carried just as much angst—fears of tripping, falling, seeing my mug dive to the floor and smash into a million pieces, splashing scalding coffee on a newborn baby nearby. How would I ever recover from the embarrassment and million dollar lawsuit that would surely follow? I felt so far removed from everything and everyone, as if watching the rest of the world from a distance and different dimension. Everyone seemed to be living life happier, faster, easier, and better, than me.

I desperately hope the clouds roll away and I soon see the sun. I *will* fight these feelings.

A Baseball Game and a Bad Rash

(for those reading this book for
just the jaw-dropping, juicy parts)

I am second-guessing what I'm about to share, fearful that it will bring more shame and embarrassment (and give you a scandalous tale to tell at your next dinner party). But omission isn't an option. To hide my darkest moments—the ugliest parts of my illness—would never paint a true picture of the pain, and would surely undermine the impact my story could ever have. This book would be an unfinished and fraudulent account, cheating myself and selling you short. So once again, here goes nothing. Or everything.

It was an impressive throw. I'd managed to hurl an object with great force and incredible aim, without knocking over a nearby lamp or the jumbo-screened TV sitting beside it. But instead of standing on a pitcher's mound in Fenway Park, I was spiralling out of control in a five-star hotel room. And in lieu of baseballs, I was throwing vibrant green apples from a complimentary fruit bowl. The only "spectator in the stands" was my horrified husband, and he wasn't eating Cracker Jacks or cheering me on. After all, I had already threatened to smash his eyeglasses, laptop, and his face. I told him if he dared to fall asleep, he would be at the mercy of my rage and might never wake. "And if you do survive to see the sunrise, you won't see me. I will be long gone," I hissed. They were all empty, idle threats.

I knew my behaviour was ridiculous, irrational, and childlike, but I didn't have the strength or desire to stop. Powerless to slow my wrecking ball from gathering steam, I gave in, fully and completely. I loved the feeling—like a rush, a hit, from the most potent drug. I wanted to take things as far as I could and scare my husband enough to feel a surge of adrenaline through *my* veins. In a tragic twist of irony, although careening out of control, at the same time, I was fully *in* control of the madness, holding my husband hostage to my hurtful words and volatile actions. I knew he wouldn't dare leave me in that state, especially knowing that the impressionable eyes and ears of our children were in the adjoining room. But it was too late... so much damage had already been done. Little did I know, my kids were listening to my horror show and forming memories of their mother that would never be forgotten.

A few more apples and impressive throws later, I decided to amp up the drama and act like a wild animal, literally. Crouched on all fours, with a few growls for added effect, I crawled across the room like a grizzly bear and perched myself under a desk. I roared again, desperately wanting and waiting for a reaction. It didn't work. My husband was silent. The "show" was over. I collapsed and began to cry uncontrollably, humiliated by my actions and my utter inability to control them. It was a relapse of epic proportions. And I knew *exactly* why.

It had started months earlier with a recurring rash on, of all places, my *face*. Within days of moving abroad, braille-like bumps had appeared and kept flaring up without rhyme or reason. In search of an instant cure and a clear-up, I sought the advice of a doctor. But after countless dietary restrictions and a few unsuccessful rounds of antibiotics, I was told, "Just live with it." Dissatisfied with my lack of a proper diagnosis, I continued searching for answers in the worst place imaginable—on the World Wide Web. Within seconds I stumbled upon a site that made a very loose link between the bumps and my bipolar medication. The suggested advice of one unreliable blogger? A ridiculously irresponsible and rapid tapering off of my meds. Foolish? Very.

I knew better. *Far* better. I was more than aware that tinkering with my dosage was as dangerous as playing with gasoline and matches; an undertaking only to be carried out under the strict supervision of a doctor. Even so, against the advice of everything and everyone I knew, my stubbornness and stupidity won out over common sense. Driven by immature vanity, I decided to take things into my own hands and become a self-appointed, self-prescribing health care professional. Committed to being responsible about my endeavour, I was sure to use the sharpest knife in the kitchen drawer to halve my pills with precision. My plan was simple: I'd reduce my dosage by a small percentage each week, until my face felt as smooth as a baby's bottom.

And now, back to the "ballgame."

As I sat and sobbed on the hotel room floor, I knew my self-monitored medical experiment had come to a crashing halt. All hopes of my rash clearing up were dashed. And I had confirmed that it wouldn't be an option to stop or even reduce my medication in the foreseeable future, if ever. I would probably be popping those little pink pills for the rest of my life.

Breathe. You're going to be okay. Breathe and remember that you've been in this place before. You've been this uncomfortable and anxious and scared, and you've survived. Breathe and know that you can survive this too. These feelings can't break you. They're painful and debilitating, but you can sit with them and eventually, they will pass. Maybe not immediately, but sometime soon, they are going to fade and when they do, you'll look back on this moment and laugh for having doubted your resilience. I know it feels unbearable right now, but keep breathing, again and again. This will pass. I promise it will pass.

-Danielle Koepke

Photo: Emma-lee Hacker

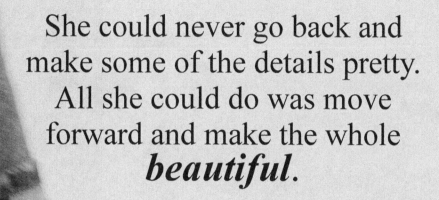

She could never go back and
make some of the details pretty.
All she could do was move
forward and make the whole
beautiful.

-Terri St. Cloud

hope and healing

Ending on a High Note

making peace with my past, my present, and *myself*

Until now, many of my words have painted a pessimistic picture of a woman who has struggled daily for decades (uphill, in the snow, barefoot, of course). It is definitely time to inject some happiness and hope, so this isn't the most depressing book you've ever read; one so heavy it's easier to put down than pick up. And, selfishly, I need to ensure two things: that my friend count doesn't dwindle and, heaven forbid, if I ever need to find myself another husband, there'll be a man out there who will still have me.

Speaking of, last time I checked, I still have a ring on my finger and a man in my bed. My husband was right. He usually is. Life with me is extremely exciting—rip-roaring, unpredictable, and, yes, at times downright dangerous. Mine is an existence of keys left dangling in doors, stovetop burners left on, and fridge and car doors left open, *overnight.* I jumpstart most of my mornings with caffeinated cereal, and stale rice casseroles are still the standard. And, you guessed it, my husband's underwear drawer is down to its last clean pair (pop the champagne and cue the background music). I run a *very* loose ship.

But my hubby's bags aren't packed. And I hope, if given the option to rewind and replay, he would pick me again. The feelings would be mutual. Despite his Type A personality and orderly way of living, I'd say,

"I do," a second time, too. Opposites really do attract. I'm wise enough to know that life without him would be nothing short of absolute chaos; I would be living on the side of a mountain, with a flock of birds in my hair, practicing my puckering techniques on a memory foam pillow. And, of course, I'd be riding a pedal-braked tricycle as my main means of transportation—a tragic result of having trashed my car's transmission years before. No need to worry, my bags aren't packed either.

The trick is to not let people know how weird you really are, until it's *too late* for them to back out.

-Unknown

Before you get too excited, I must admit I still have days when my luck runs out before it has even begun. Handsome male cashiers always seem to start their shifts just in time to ring through my order, which, of course, consists of a lifetime supply of feminine hygiene products and a few highly contagious rash ointments. (Self-checkout, *please.*) And just when things can't seem to get any worse, my not-so-private purchases will end up needing a very public price check. Did I mention Murphy's Law? It will be proven alive and well when I notice my ex-boyfriend standing next in line, deciding to finally break his decades-long silence, "Julie, is that you?" Yes. Yes, I think it is.

But all things considered, I've made *major* progress. The number of days when I bound out of bed and brush my teeth far outnumber those when I cower under the covers. The world is out there for me and, most of the time, I believe it. I'm living life to the fullest, in first person, from the front row.

I'm doing my best to retrain my brain, tweak my thought process, and adjust the filter through which I sift others' words and actions. I'm fighting first instincts and switching default settings; pushing through all those moments when I take unreturned emails, and almost everything else, straight to the heart and in the worst possible ways.

Don't believe *everything* you think.

My thoughts of unworthiness are lies, and I've stopped believing most of them. Irrational and insecure actions are being tamed too. I am suppressing sudden urges to delete my manuscript, defriend my entire social media network, and abandon the 50,000 projects I've begun. I now know it's only a matter of a few deep breaths and days until I'm burning brightly again, harnessing my explosive creativity, and scrolling through an inbox of returned messages from friends who only needed to wake from a coma or finish grooming their pets.

I am no longer swinging from one extreme to another. I can recognize warning signs and stop wrecking balls from gathering steam. Thankfully, adrenaline rushes now only come from discovering free furniture by the roadside or designer shirt sales (white silk, of course). My outbursts of anger are a less common occurrence and no longer a way of releasing pent-up frustration from hiding behind a fake smile. And just in case you were wondering, there's no need to remind me that hotel fruit bowls are for consumption, not sport. So, with the exception of a sink full of last year's dishes, I'm a responsible adult—calm, cool, and in control. I am a far better wife, mom, daughter, sister, and friend than ever before.

Life offers no guarantees. None, whatsoever. And surely, to the dismay of my parents and husband at times, it offers no return policies, either. It can only be faced head-on, day by day, and, at times, minute to minute. As a knob-kneed little girl, I asked Santa for my two front teeth, an Easy-Bake oven, and a first kiss before my fortieth birthday. I dreamed of throwing a bridal bouquet, yelling for the home team, and bowling at my friends' birthday parties. No, having a mental illness never topped my Christmas wish list. Never in a million years did I picture myself throwing fruit, yelling at my husband, or "lawn bowling" at midnight. I have been dealt a few cards and thrown a few curve balls that could have destroyed me, and at times almost did. But I found my footing and survived. I *am* surviving; dare I quietly and cautiously say, even *thriving*. And I wouldn't change a single thing. No, I wouldn't go back and trade in my troubles... heaven only knows what I might be dealt instead.

I'm thankful for my struggle
because, without it,
I wouldn't have stumbled
upon my *strength*.

-Alexandra Elle

Thankfully, my bipolarity is no longer a bombshell admission or headline story in my life. My initial feelings of shame and brokenness have faded, and I finally view my disorder through my friends' eyes as something I *have*, not something I *am*. It doesn't define my relationships or me. I am more than my mental illness. *So much more.* My disorder is an added bonus feature to the already complex, dramatic, passionate, square-pegged person I am. I choose to view my wild creativity and bursts of rocket-fuelled energy as gifts that can be tamed and harnessed to pursue my wildest dreams and accomplish amazing goals. The positive things in my life far outnumber the negatives; I need only remind myself which should hold the most weight. I'm making the most of my best parts and managing the worst.

I look to the future with hope and excitement, ready to unlock my front door and race outside, whether I'm wearing socks and sandals or stilettos. Most Sunday mornings you will still find me in a church pew, with a Bible in hand and my husband by my side (who may or may not be wearing clean underwear, if any at all). On the way home, I'll be sure to stop at a trendy café for a 360-degree custom-made coffee (under the name Maximiliènne-Francesca, of course). And then, maybe, just maybe, I'll squeeze in a surprise appearance and an off-tune karaoke performance (of a Bryan Adams song, of course) at Dieter's (insurance guy, remember?) birthday party.

But if I wake with blue skies clouded over and the sun nowhere in sight, I'll take a few deep breaths, pull my granny panties up sky-high, and *wait*. I will be patient and wait for the light to return, because it *always* does.

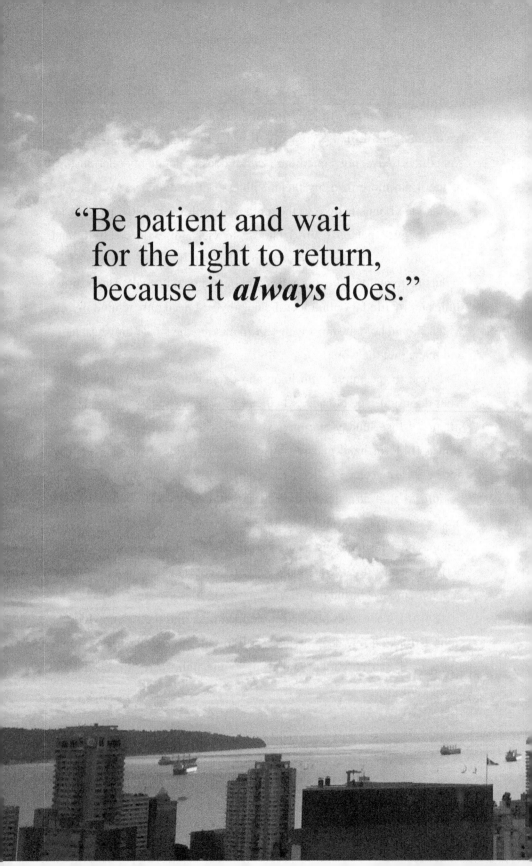

"Be patient and wait
for the light to return,
because it *always* does."

"Opening up to others
is *always* a risk.

One that I thought was *worth taking*."

Photo: Emma-lee Hacker

about the author.

As a fireball wife and mother, Julie enjoys juggling her time between caring for her family of five and pursuing her many creative interests. Aside from word-slinging, her passions include travelling, painting, people-watching, photography, thrifting, and all aspects of art and interior design. After spending three years living in Karlsruhe, Germany, Julie is now back in her hometown of Vancouver, Canada. She continues to tuck herself away in cafés and write, using her life experiences and far too much coffee as fuel. It is her greatest hope that her words will change others and the world in the most unexpected and inspiring ways.

In a world full of fear, be courageous.
In a world full of lies, be honest.
In a world where few care, be compassionate.
In a world full of phonies, be yourself.
Because the world sees you.
The world hopes for you.
The world is inspired by you.
The world can be better because of *you*.

-Doe Zantamata

Photo: Emma-lee Hacker

Made in the USA
Monee, IL
21 July 2020

36839995R00118